THE
SELF-
AWARE
LEADER

BOOKS BY DR. JOHN C. MAXWELL CAN TEACH YOU HOW TO BE A REAL SUCCESS

RELATIONSHIPS

25 Ways to Win with People
Be a People Person
Becoming a Person of Influence
Everyone Communicates,
*   Few Connect*
The Power of Influence
Relationships 101
The Treasure of a Friend
Winning with People

ATTITUDE

Attitude 101
The Difference Maker
Failing Forward
The Power of Attitude
Sometimes You Win—
*   Sometimes You Learn*
Success Is a Choice
Think on These Things
The Winning Attitude

EQUIPPING

The 15 Invaluable Laws of Growth
The 17 Essential Qualities
*   of a Team Player*
The 17 Indisputable Laws
*   of Teamwork*
Beyond Talent
Developing the Leaders Around You
Equipping 101
How Successful People Grow
How Successful People Think
My Dream Map
No Limits
Your Road Map for Success

LEADERSHIP

The 5 Levels of Leadership
The 21 Indispensable
*   Qualities of a Leader*
The 21 Irrefutable Laws
*   of Leadership*
The 21 Most Powerful Minutes
*   in a Leader's Day*
The 360 Degree Leader
Developing the Leader
*   Within You 2.0*
Good Leaders Ask Great Questions
How to Lead When Your Boss
*   Can't (Or Won't)*
Leadershift
The Power of Leadership

THE SELF- AWARE LEADER

Play to Your Strengths and
Unleash Your Team

JOHN C. MAXWELL

HARPERCOLLINS
LEADERSHIP

AN IMPRINT OF HARPERCOLLINS

PUBLISHING

Derived from material previously published in *Leadership Gold: Lessons I've Learned from a Lifetime of Leading.*

Published by HarperCollins Leadership, an imprint of HarperCollins Focus LLC.

Published in association with Yates & Yates, www.yates2.com.

ISBN 978-0-7852-6664-8 (HC)
ISBN 978-0-7852-8819-0 (eBook)

Printed in the United States of America

23 24 25 26 27 LBC 8 7 6 5 4

CONTENTS

....

ACKNOWLEDGMENT

....

I want to say thank you to Charlie Wetzel and the rest of the team who assisted me with the formation and publication of this book. And to the people in my organizations who support it. You all add incredible value to me, which allows me to add value to others. Together, we're making a difference!

INTRODUCTION

....

What sabotages more leadership efforts, holds back more good teams, and derails more leaders' careers than anything else? Lack of self-awareness! When leaders don't see themselves clearly, are unaware of their strengths and weaknesses, or fail to recognize their negative interactions with their team members, they limit their influence and undermine their own effectiveness.

When I talk with the finest executive coaches in my organization, they tell me that lack of self-awareness is the single greatest problem they see in the leaders they coach. Sadly, they have observed that poor self-awareness is as common in the C-suite as it is among entry-level leaders.

How do you know whether you are self-aware as a leader? Perhaps you don't! All leaders have blind spots.

If yours prevent you from seeing yourself clearly, you won't be aware of it. So you need to get help. I've written this book to help you and get you on the journey to better self-awareness. I'll ask you questions to get you thinking, point out where common blind spots lie, and give you strategies to grow and change. You will become better at leading yourself, become more aware of your strengths and weaknesses, and—most important—improve your interactions with the people on your team, which is where most leaders who lack self-awareness experience breakdowns.

If you're new to leadership, the following chapters will help you get a better start on your leadership journey. If you're an experienced leader, this book will help you fine-tune your leadership. No leader can be too self-aware. The better you know and manage yourself, the better you will be able to lead and serve your team.

ONE

BECOME GOOD AT LEADING YOURSELF

....

What has been your greatest challenge as a leader? Your mind may go to a season of struggle for your organization, a particularly difficult problem you had to deal with, or a person who betrayed you or caused your team to fail. But if you're really gut-level honest, the greatest challenge leaders face is leading themselves.

I know that's always been my greatest challenge as a leader. I also think that's true for all leaders regardless of who they lead or what they accomplish. We sometimes think about accomplished leaders from history and assume that they had it all together. But if we really examine their lives, whether we're looking at King David, George Washington, Mahatma Gandhi, or Martin Luther King, Jr., we can see that they struggled to lead themselves well too. That's why I say that the toughest person to lead is always yourself. It's like Walt Kelly exclaimed in his *Pogo* cartoon strip: "We have met the enemy and he is us."[1] That's why you need to become good at leading yourself.

Acknowledging that leading myself is a challenge brings back some painful memories. Many of my leadership breakdowns have been personal breakdowns. In a leadership career that has spanned more than five decades, I've made plenty of mistakes, but I have experienced only four major leadership crises. And I'm sorry to say that all of them were my fault.

The first occurred in 1970, just two years into my first official leadership position. After two years of work, I had won over many people and there was a lot going on. However, one day I realized that my organization had no direction. Why? Because I lacked the ability to prioritize correctly and bring focus to my leadership. As a young leader, I didn't yet understand that activity does not necessarily equal accomplishment. As a result, my people, following my example, wandered in the wilderness for sixteen months. In the end, I didn't really lead them anywhere.

The next crisis came in 1979. At that time I felt pulled in two directions. I had been successful in my second leadership position, but I also realized that if I was going to reach a broader audience, which I felt was the right thing to try to do, I would have to leave the organization I had been a part of for the first twelve years of my career. My uncertainty and the personal changes that I was dealing with negatively impacted the organization I led. I became unfocused, and my vision for the organization became cloudy. My passion and energy also began to wane. Leaders who aren't focused aren't as effective as they could be. As a result, we weren't moving forward as effectively as we could have.

The third occurred in 1991 when I was overloaded with work and my life was out of balance. Because I had been leading my organization successfully for ten years, I thought I could take a few shortcuts to make things easier for me. I made three difficult decisions in rapid succession without doing proper due diligence or taking the time needed to process everyone in my organization through my decisions. What a mistake! As a result, the people were not prepared for the decisions and reacted badly. The trust that it had taken me a decade to build was undermined. To make matters worse, when the people who questioned my decisions balked at following my lead, I became impatient. I angrily thought, *What is their problem? Why don't they "get it" and get on with it?*

Within a few weeks, I realized that the problem wasn't them. It was me. I ended up having to apologize to everyone for my attitude.

The fourth occurred in 2001 and involved a staff member whom I needed to let go. I delayed the decision when I shouldn't have, and my unwillingness to make that difficult decision cost me many dollars and some key personnel. Once again, I was the source of the problem.

JUDGE FOR YOURSELF

If you want a better team in a better organization that produces better results, you need to become better at leading yourself. Most leaders need to worry less about the competition, because other people aren't more successful. As leaders, we often hold ourselves back. Why?

We Don't See Ourselves as We See Others

My years counseling others taught me something important: people seldom see themselves realistically. They aren't self-aware. Human nature seems to endow us with the ability to size up everybody in the world except ourselves. That's why in my book *Winning with People* I start with the Mirror Principle, which advises, "The First Person We Must Examine Is Ourselves."

4

If you don't look at yourself realistically, you will
never understand where
your personal difficulties
lie. You won't recognize
your strengths and weak-
nesses. You won't find and
correct your blind spots. And if you can't see all these
things, you won't be able to lead yourself effectively.

> **Human nature seems
> to endow us with
> the ability to size up
> everybody in the world
> except ourselves.**

We Are Harder on Others Than We Are on Ourselves

Most people use two totally different sets of criteria
for judging themselves versus others. We tend to judge
others according to their *actions* and *results*. We often
see our observations as very cut-and-dried. However,
we judge ourselves by our *intentions*. Even when we do
the wrong thing or the results are terrible, if we believe
our motives were good, we let ourselves off the hook.
And we are often willing to do that over and over before
requiring ourselves to change. That doesn't make us
effective leaders.

KEYS TO LEADING YOURSELF BETTER

The truth is that to be successful in any endeavor, we need
to learn how to get out of our own way. That's as true for

leaders as it is for anyone else. Because I have known for many years that leading myself is my toughest job, I have taken steps to help become better at it. By practicing the following four strategies, I have tried to lead myself well as a prerequisite to leading others. You can use them to help you become better at leading yourself.

1. Learn Followership

Bishop Fulton J. Sheen remarked, "Civilization is always in danger when those who have never learned to obey are given the right to command." Only a leader who has followed well knows how to lead others well. Good leadership requires an understanding of the world that followers live in. Connecting with the people on your team becomes possible because you have walked in their shoes. You know what it means to be under authority and thus have a better sense of how authority should be exercised. In contrast, leaders who have never followed well or submitted to authority tend to be prideful, unrealistic, rigid, and autocratic.

> "Civilization is always in danger when those who have never learned to obey are given the right to command."
> —BISHOP FULTON J. SHEEN

If those words describe your leadership, you need to do some soul-searching. Arrogant leaders are rarely effective in the long run. They alienate their followers, their colleagues, and their leaders. Learn to submit to another person's leadership and to follow well, and you will become a humbler—and more effective—leader.

2. Develop Self-Discipline

It's said that one day Frederick the Great of Prussia was walking on the outskirts of Berlin when he encountered a very old man walking ramrod straight in the opposite direction.

"Who are you?" Frederick asked his subject.

"I am a king," replied the old man.

"A king!" laughed Frederick. "Over what kingdom do you reign?"

"Over myself," was the proud old man's reply.

Each of us must become the "monarch" of our own lives. We are responsible for ruling our actions and decisions. To make consistently good decisions, to take the right action when needed, and to refrain from the wrong actions requires character and self-discipline. To do otherwise is to lose control of ourselves—to do or say things we regret, to miss opportunities we are given, to spend ourselves into debt. As King Solomon

> When we are foolish, we want to conquer the world. When we are wise, we want to conquer ourselves.

remarked, "The rich rule over the poor, and the borrower is servant to the lender."[2]

In "Decision of Character," British essayist John Foster writes, "A man without decision of character can never be said to belong to himself. He belongs to whatever can make a captive of him." When we are foolish, we want to conquer the world. When we are wise, we want to conquer ourselves. That begins when we do what we should no matter how we feel about it.

3. Practice Patience

The leaders I know tend to be impatient. They look ahead, think ahead, and want to move ahead. And that can be good. Being one step ahead makes you a leader. However, that can also be bad. If you're out front but you're impatient with your team, you may resent them instead of encouraging them to come along with you. That makes you less effective as a leader.

Few worthwhile things in life come quickly. There is no such thing as instant greatness or instant maturity. We are used to instant oatmeal, instant coffee, and microwave popcorn. But becoming a leader doesn't happen overnight. Microwave leaders don't have any staying power. Leadership is more of a Crock-Pot proposition. It takes time, but the end product is worth the wait.

Leaders need to remember that the point of leading is not to cross the finish line first. It's to take people across the finish line *with* you. For that reason, leaders must deliberately slow their pace, stay connected to their people, enlist others to help fulfill the vision, and keep people going. You can't do that if you're running too far ahead of your people. Or have a bad attitude about their pace.

4. Seek Accountability

People who lead themselves well know a secret: they can't trust themselves. Good leaders know that power can be seductive, and they understand their own fallibility. To be a leader and deny this is to put yourself in danger.

Over the years, I've read about many leaders who tried to be good people yet failed ethically in their leadership. Can you guess what most of them had in common? They thought it could never happen to them. There was a false sense of security. They thought they were incapable of ruining their lives and destroying their teams or organizations.

Learning that was very sobering to me, because I shared the same attitude. I thought I was above such possibilities, and when I realized I had the same blind spot they did, it scared me. At that moment, I made two decisions: First, I will not trust myself. Second, I will become accountable to someone other than myself. I believe those decisions have helped keep me on track and able to lead myself and others.

> "When you see a good man, think of emulating him; when you see a bad man, examine your heart."
> —CHINESE PROVERB

Lack of accountability in our personal life will certainly lead to problems in our public life. We saw that time and time again with high-profile CEOs a few years ago. A Chinese proverb says, "When you see a good man, think of emulating him; when you see a bad man, examine your heart."

Many people think of accountability as a willingness to explain their actions. I believe that effective accountability begins *before* we take action. It starts with getting advice from others. Many leaders find this difficult, and sometimes their openness to advice is developed only in stages as they become better at leading themselves. It often goes like this:

I don't want advice.
I don't object to advice.
I welcome advice.
I actively seek advice.
I often follow the advice I'm given.

The willingness to seek and accept advice is a great indicator of accountability. And of a leader who is maturing and improving.

Leading yourself well means that you hold yourself to a higher standard of accountability than others do. Why? Because you are held responsible not only for your own actions but also for those of the people you lead. Leadership is a trust, not a right. For that reason, we must "fix" ourselves earlier than others may be required to. We must always seek to do what's right, no matter how high we rise or how powerful we become. It's a struggle we never outgrow.

When Harry S. Truman was thrust into the presidency upon the death of Franklin Roosevelt, Sam Rayburn gave him some fatherly advice: "From here on out you're going to have lots of people around you. They'll try to put a wall around you and cut you off from any ideas but theirs. They'll tell you what a great man you are, Harry. But you and I both know you ain't."[3]

Recently I participated in a conference call with board members of an organization who had to step in and hold a leader accountable for wrong actions he had taken. It was a sad experience. He will probably lose his leadership position. He has already lost his board's respect. If only he had devoted more time and attention to becoming better at leading himself, the board's actions might not have become necessary. After the

> "Nothing so conclusively proves a man's ability to lead others as what he does from day to day to lead himself."
> —THOMAS J. WATSON

call I thought to myself, *When the leader doesn't inspect himself, the people don't respect him.*

Thomas J. Watson, the former chairman of IBM, said, "Nothing so conclusively proves a man's ability to lead others as what he does from day to day to lead himself." How true. The smallest group you will ever lead is you, a group of one. That is the most important one you will ever lead. If you do that well, then you will earn the right to lead even bigger and stronger groups.

THE SELF-AWARE LEADER'S
QUESTIONS FOR REFLECTION

How willing am I to be honest with myself about how I need to change to become better at self-leadership? What colleague, trusted friend, or mentor would be able and willing to point out how and where I need to change and give me advice? Will I make that appointment right now?

_____

_____

_____

_____

_____

_____

_____

_____

_____

_____

_____

TWO

KNOW AND WORK WITHIN YOUR STRENGTHS

....

Can you remember the first lesson you ever learned about leadership? I can. It came from my dad. He used to tell my brother, my sister, and me, "Find out what you do well and keep on doing it." That wasn't just casual advice. He and my mother made it their mission to help us discover our strengths and start developing them before we were old enough to leave home and go out on our own.

Dad also reinforced that advice by living it. One of his favorite sayings was, "This one thing I do." He had an uncanny ability to remain focused within his areas of strength. That, coupled with his determination to finish what he started, served him well throughout his career and into retirement up to the day he died. He stayed in his strengths. It is one of the reasons he has always been the greatest inspiration for my life.

SEARCHING FOR STRENGTHS

When I started my career, I was committed to finding my strengths and working within them. However, I was frustrated for my first few years in leadership. Like many inexperienced leaders, I tried doing many different things to discover what I could do well. In addition, people's expectations for what I should do and how I would lead impacted what I did. Those actions did not always match my strengths. My role and responsibilities sometimes required that I perform tasks for which I possessed neither talent nor skill. I was often ineffective as a result. It took me several years to sort all this out, find my strengths, and recruit and develop other people to compensate for my weaknesses.

If you are a young leader and you are still uncertain about where your strengths lie, don't get discouraged. Be patient and keep working it out. Here's what I know: whether you're just starting out or if you are at the peak of your career, the more you know your strengths and work within them, the more successful you will be.

DEFINING PERSONAL SUCCESS

I've heard many definitions of success from many people over the years. In fact, I've embraced different definitions myself at different stages of my life. But in the last fifteen years, I have zeroed in on a definition that I think captures success for all people, no matter where they live or what they want to do. I believe success is:

> Knowing your purpose in life,
> Growing to your maximum potential, and
> Sowing seeds that benefit others.

If you are able to do those three things, you are successful. However, none of them is possible unless you know and work within your strengths.

I love the story of a group of neighborhood boys who built a clubhouse and formed their own club. When the grown-ups were told who had been selected for which office, they were astonished to hear that a four-year-old had been elected president.

"That boy must be a born leader," one dad observed.

"How did it happen that all you bigger boys voted for him?"

"Well, you see, Dad," his son replied, "he can't very well be secretary because he doesn't know how to read or write. He couldn't be treasurer, because he can't count. He would never do for sergeant at arms because he's too little to throw anybody out. If we didn't choose him for anything, he'd feel bad. So we made him president."

Real life, of course, doesn't work that way. Good leaders don't become effective by default or appointed by pity. They must be intentional and work from their strengths.

> People's purpose in life is always connected to their giftedness.

Whenever I mentor people and help them discover their purpose, I always encourage them to start the process by discovering their strengths, not exploring their shortcomings. Why? Because people's purpose in life is always connected to their giftedness. It always works that way. You will not be called to do something that you have no talent for. You will discover your purpose by finding and remaining in your strengths.

Similarly, you cannot grow to your maximum potential if you continually work outside of your strengths. Improvement is always related to ability. The greater your natural ability, the greater your potential for improvement. I've known people who thought that reaching their potential would come from shoring up their weaknesses. But do you know what happens when you spend all your time working on your weaknesses and never developing your strengths? If you work really hard, you might claw your way all the way up to mediocrity! But you'll never get beyond it. Nobody admires or rewards mediocrity.

The final piece of the puzzle—living a life that benefits others—always depends upon us giving our best, not our worst. You can't change the world by giving only leftovers or by performing with mediocrity. Only your best will add value to others and help them to do their best.

FINDING YOUR OWN STRENGTHS

British poet and lexicographer Samuel Johnson said, "Almost every man wastes part of his life in attempts to display qualities which he does not possess." If you have an image in your mind of what talents a leader must have, yet you do not possess them, then you will have a difficult

> "Almost every man wastes part of his life in attempts to display qualities which he does not possess."
> —SAMUEL JOHNSON

time finding your true strengths. You need to discover and develop who *you* are, and bring the strengths you have to your leadership. Here are a few suggestions to help you:

1. Ask, "What Am I Doing Well?"

People who reach their potential spend less time asking, "What am I doing right?" and more time asking, "What am I doing well?" The first is a moral question; the second is a talent question. You should always strive to do what's right. But doing what's right doesn't tell you anything about your talent. What skills and abilities do you have that are way beyond average? These strengths should be what you develop.

2. Get Specific About Your Strengths

When we consider our strengths, we tend to think too broadly. Peter Drucker, the father of modern management, writes, "The great mystery isn't that people do things badly but that they occasionally do a few things well. The only thing that is universal is incompetence. Strength is always specific! Nobody ever commented, for example, that the great violinist Jascha Heifetz probably couldn't play the trumpet well."

The more specific you can get about your strengths, the better the chance you can find your "sweet spot." Why be on the fringes of your strength zone when you have a chance to be right in the center? What are your strengths within your strengths?

3. Listen for What Others Praise

Many times we take our talents for granted. We think because we can do something well, anyone can. That's often not true. How can you tell when you're overlooking a skill or talent? Listen to what others say. When you're working in areas of weakness, few people will show interest. They won't compliment you. In contrast, your strengths will capture the attention of others and draw them to you. If others are continually praising you in a particular area, identify it, examine it, and start developing it.

4. Check Out the Competition

You don't want to spend all your time comparing yourself to others; that's not healthy. But you don't want to waste your time doing something that others do much better that you do. Former GE CEO Jack Welch asserts, "If you don't have a competitive advantage, don't compete."[1] People don't pay for average. If you don't have the talent to do something better than others, find something else to do that leverages your abilities.

> "Discover your uniqueness, then discipline yourself to develop it."
> —JIM SUNDBERG

If you're not sure how to judge your own abilities, ask yourself the following questions:

- Is someone else doing what I am doing?
- Are they doing it well?
- Are they doing it better than I am?
- Can I become better than they are?
- If I do become better, what will be the result?
- If I don't become better, what will be the result?

The answer to the last question is: you lose. Why? Because your "competition" is working in their strengths and you aren't!

Former all-star baseball catcher Jim Sundberg advised, "Discover your uniqueness, then discipline yourself to develop it." That's what I've tried to do. Many years ago I realized that one of my strengths was communicating. People have always been motivated when they hear me speak. After a while, I received many opportunities to speak at events with other motivational speakers. At first it was intimidating because they were so good. But as I listened to them, the thing I kept asking myself was, "What can I do that will set me apart from them?" I felt it might not be possible for me to be better than they were, but it would be possible for me to be different. Over time I discovered and developed that difference. I would strive to be a motivational *teacher*, not just a motivational *speaker*. I wanted people not only to enjoy what I shared but also to be able to apply what I taught to their lives. For more than three decades, I have disciplined my life to develop that uniqueness. It's my niche—my strength zone.

SELF-AWARE LEADERS KNOW AND DEVELOP THE STRENGTHS OF THEIR PEOPLE

Whenever you see people who are successful in their work, you can rest assured that they are working in their strengths. But that's not enough if you want to be successful as a leader. Good leaders who are self-aware don't just help themselves. They help the people on their team to find their strengths, and they empower them to work in those strengths. In fact, the best leaders are characterized by their ability to recognize the special abilities and limitations of their people and fit them into the jobs where they will do best.

Sadly, most people are not working in their areas of strength and therefore are not reaching their potential.

> "Organizations exist to make people's strengths effective and their weaknesses irrelevant. And this is the work of effective leaders."
> —FRANCES HESSELBEIN

The Gallup organization conducted research on 1.7 million people in the workplace. According to their findings, only twenty percent of employees feel that their strengths are in play every day in the work setting.[2] In my opinion, that is largely the fault of their leaders. Many leaders fail to help their people find their strengths and place them in the organization where their strengths can be an asset to the company.

In her book *Hesselbein on Leadership*, Frances Hesselbein, President and CEO of the Frances Hesselbein Leadership Institute at the University of Pennsylvania, writes, "Peter Drucker reminds us that organizations exist to make people's strengths effective and their weaknesses irrelevant. And this is the work of effective leaders. Drucker also tells us that there may be born leaders but there are far too few to depend on them."[3]

If you desire to be an effective leader, you must increase your ability to develop people in their areas of strength. How do you do that?

Become Secure in Your Own Leadership

When you become self-aware as a leader, you become more secure as a leader. You know your strengths, and you don't have to prove them. You know your weaknesses, and you don't want to hide them. You are who you are, you work in your strengths, and you are willing to leverage them to help others develop theirs.

23

Study and Know the People on Your Team

Get to know the members of your team. What are their strengths and weaknesses? Whom do they relate to on the team? Are they growing and do they have more growth potential in the area in which they're working? Is their attitude an asset or a liability? Do they love what they do and are they doing it well? These are questions that you must learn the answers to.

Communicate to Individuals How They Fit on the Team

Tell people what strengths they bring to the table. Tell them how they complement the other members of the team. Figure out what they need from the other players that will complement their weaknesses, and communicate that. The more they know about how they fit on a team, the more they will desire to make the most of their fit and maximize their contribution.

Communicate to All Team Members How Each Player Fits on the Team

It's obvious that you can't have a winning team without teamwork. However, not every leader actively works to help team members work together. Don't fall into that trap. Take responsibility for communicating to all the players how all the people fit together and what strengths they bring for their role. The more you do this, the more people will value and respect one another.

Emphasize Completing One Another Above Competing with One Another

Healthy competition between teammates is good. It presses them to do their best. But in the end, team members need to work together for the sake of the team, not only for themselves. Help everyone on your team to keep this in perspective.

———

To some leaders, the idea of focusing almost entirely on strengths seems counterintuitive. Several years ago I was spending a day with leaders of several companies, and one of the subjects I addressed was the importance of staying in your strengths. I repeatedly encouraged them not to work with their areas of weakness related to ability. At the end of one of the sessions, a CEO pushed back against the idea. The example he used was that of Tiger Woods.

"When Tiger plays a bad round of golf," he observed, "he goes straight to the driving range and practices for hours. You see, John, he's working on his weaknesses."

"No," I replied, "he's working on his strengths. Tiger is a great golfer, one of the best in the world. What is he doing? He's practicing *golf* shots. He's not practicing accounting or music or basketball. He is working on a weakness within his strength zone, which is golf. That will always produce positive results."

Working on a weakness in your strength zone will always produce greater results than working on a strength in a weak area. I love golf, but if I practice golf shots, I will never greatly improve. Why? Because I'm an average golfer. Practice won't make perfect—it will make permanent! If I want to make progress, I need to keep working on my leadership and communication. Those are my strengths.

What are yours? Are you spending time in them? If so, then you are making an investment into your success.

THE SELF-AWARE LEADER'S
QUESTIONS FOR REFLECTION

Where am I strongest? What are my top three strengths? Where am I weakest? Who on my team can I help using my strengths? Who can I ask to help me where I'm weakest?

_____

_____

_____

_____

_____

_____

_____

_____

_____

_____

_____

THREE

PUT YOUR TEAM AHEAD OF YOUR OWN CAREER ADVANCEMENT

....

When I first started in my career, I thought leadership was a race. My goal was to prove myself and improve my ranking. I worked hard. And each year I couldn't wait as the annual report came out with the stats for every leader within our national organization. I would compare my numbers with everyone else's. I charted my progress. I checked to see whom I had overtaken. I noted which leaders ahead of me were within reach.

Every year I inched closer to the top, and it gave me a great sense of satisfaction. I was climbing!

However, there were significant problems with my thinking. I was working under two major misconceptions: First, I thought my leadership title made me a leader. Second, I thought that climbing the ladder in my career was a higher priority than connecting with people and advancing the team. The bottom line was that I didn't realize that leadership is relational more than positional, and helping the team win is much more important than winning personally.

I had my first wake-up call when I led my first board meeting. I had the "rights" to operate as the leader, but not the relationships. The people in the meeting listened to me politely, but they didn't follow me. They followed Claude, a farmer who had been around since before I was born. Watching people follow based on the relationship instead of the position was at first a frustration for me. It took me nearly a decade to understand that people do not care how much you know until they know how much you care. I wish somebody had told me that sooner. Perhaps they did, but I was too busy trying to get ahead. As a result, I wasn't connecting with people, and I was endangering my team.

> **People do not care how much you know until they know how much you care.**

That's not to say that climbing is all wrong. You can't create progress by staying on a plateau. Leaders are naturally wired to climb. They can be aggressive. Good leaders initiate. They see opportunities and seek them before others do. Most leaders are competitive, and getting to the top is part of their DNA. So the question for leaders is not, "Should you try to get to the top?" Two better questions are, "How should you try to get there?" and "Who should you take with you?" Getting to the top without connecting with our people at best allows us to lead people without their allegiance. At worst it undermines our leadership and makes the team suffer.

CHANGE IN ATTITUDE

Over the years I have watched many young leaders who climbed without connecting. They placed the positional aspect of leadership ahead of the relational one, playing a form of the kid's game king of the hill—knocking down others to keep themselves on top. I think many young leaders starting out don't realize that the game of leadership can be played any other way. But there comes a point in the experience of all leaders when they become confronted with a choice. Are they going to compete at all costs to climb over others to make sure they get to the top, or are they going to connect with others and help them climb to the top with them?

I remember well facing this decision. Early in my first pastorate, I wanted to teach my congregation how to manage their time, talents, and finances. I knew that this kind of stewardship of what we have is important, but because of my lack of experience, I had no resources to draw upon to help me. I went to a bookstore in Bedford, Indiana, in search of material, and I could find *nothing* that applied. As I drove home, I knew I could choose to give up, or I could try to develop ideas and resources of my own. I knew it would be a very difficult and time-consuming task, but I was willing to give it a try.

It took me months to develop material out of what felt like thin air, but after a lot of extra hours of preparation, I was ready to launch my first "stewardship month." And to my great delight, it was a tremendous success! Our attendance grew, our finances increased, and people began volunteering. It was a transformative experience for our small church and a huge momentum maker. And the results could be seen in the annual report when the church's numbers jumped dramatically.

The word soon got out that something exciting had happened at our church. And it wasn't long before other church leaders were asking me to teach them how to do what I had done. In that moment, I had a dilemma. What would I do? Would I keep what I had learned to myself, not sharing it with my colleagues? That way, I could keep my edge and climb above many of them on the leadership ladder! Or would I share with them all that I had learned so that they could also be successful? After all, all pastors are supposed to be playing for the same team.

I'm ashamed to admit that I wrestled with this decision for many days. I really wanted to keep my advantage and continue advancing my own career. But I finally decided not to hoard what I had. I chose to share it with others. What amazed me was how fulfilled I felt after helping those leaders learn how to teach steward-ship to their congregations. And it created relational connections.

For the next twenty-four years, I led an annual stewardship month with my people. And every year after I was done, I made my lessons available to other leaders so that they could use them too. It ended up connecting me with a lot of other leaders around the country. What's ironic is that by maintaining an abun-dance mindset and sharing what I had with others, I actually climbed in reputation nationally as a leader.

WHICH KIND OF LEADER ARE YOU?

If you want to be an effective leader, you must take responsibility for helping your team win. How can you do that? By connecting with team members, getting to know who they are, learning to care about them, and finding ways for them to succeed individually and as a team.

Most leaders naturally fall into either the climber or connector camp. They are either focused on advancing in their career or connecting with their team and helping them advance. Which type of leader are you? Take a look at some of the differences between climbers and connectors:

Climbers Think Vertical—Connectors Think Horizontal

Climbers are always acutely aware of who is ahead of them and who is behind them in the standings or on the organizational chart. They are the way I was as a young leader—reading the reports to see where they rank so that they can get ahead. To them, moving up is very important, and the idea of moving down is unacceptable. Connectors, on the other hand, are focused on moving over to where their team members are and helping them. They think more about who is on the journey with them and how they can help them. They put the good of the team ahead of their own personal gain.

Climbers Focus on Position—Connectors Focus on Relationships

Because climbers are always thinking about moving up, they are often focused on their position. However,

> **Positional people desire to climb the ladder; relational people are more focused on building bridges.**

connectors are more focused on relationships. Unlike positional people who desire to climb the ladder, relational people are more focused on building bridges.

Climbers Value Competition—Connectors Value Cooperation

Climbers see nearly everything as a competition. For some, that can mean trying to win at all costs. For others it can mean seeing success as an enjoyable game. Either way, they want to end up on top. Connectors, however, are more interested in using their relationships with others to foster cooperation. They see working together toward a greater goal as a win.

Climbers Seek Power—Connectors Seek Partnerships

If your mindset is always to win, then you naturally want power because it helps you to climb faster and reach the top more quickly. However, climbing the leadership ladder is really a solo endeavor. Working alone pales in significance to what you can do with a team of people. The way to create really high-powered teams is to form partnerships, which is what connectors are more likely to do.

Climbers Build Their Image—Connectors Build Consensus

To advance their careers and climb the organizational ladder, most leaders depend on others to promote them. Because of that, many climbers worry greatly about their image. They want to *appear* strong. They want to *appear* in charge. They want to *appear* successful. And some will do anything to maintain that image. Connectors, on the other hand, are more concerned with getting everyone on the same page so that they can work together. They seek common ground. They build consensus. They worry more about the unity of the team than standing out from the crowd.

> **Connectors worry more about the unity of the team than standing out from the crowd.**

Climbers Want to Stand Apart—Connectors Want to Stand Together

Climbers want to distinguish themselves from everybody else in the organization. Like racers, they want to create separation—to leave everyone else in the dust. Connectors, on the other hand, find ways to get closer to other people, to join with others so that they can stand together.

THE SHIFT TOWARD CONNECTION

I have perhaps painted climbers in an unflattering light. I don't mean to do that. After all, my natural inclination is to be a climber. But success in leadership comes to those who embrace the positive aspects of ambition along with the positive characteristics of connecting. If you're naturally a climber as I am, then focus on building positive relationships with others, especially your team members. If you look at the top reasons people fail at work, you will find that they are frequently due to an inability to get along well with others. In a recent article in *Inc.*, executive John White wrote about the top seven reasons people lose their jobs. Five of the seven were related to difficulties in getting along with others. People skills are important for success at every level.[1]

If you climb without connecting, you may advance your career, but few people will want to work with you. And you won't have many friends at work. A leader's goal should be to make friends *and* gain authority. So if you're a climber, you may need to temper your competitiveness and slow down to build relationships. Judith Tobin suggests the value of five qualities that can assist you to connect with others:

- **Appreciation** allows for differences in people and considers them interesting.

- **Sensitivity** understands personal feelings and quickly takes into account the moods of others.
- **Consistency** has the quality of being "real," not phony, and gives only sincere compliments.
- **Security** doesn't try to be "top dog"; it knows that helping others win isn't a loss for you.
- **Humor** laughs at itself; it is not overly sensitive.

This doesn't mean that connecting is everything. If you connect well but possess little desire to improve yourself or your career, people may like you, but you may not possess the drive or develop the authority to actually accomplish anything. If you're a natural connector, work to increase your energy and intensify your sense of purpose and urgency. The most effective leaders always manage to balance both connecting and climbing while advancing their teams.

VALUE THE TEAM

If you look back at the history of management and leadership ideas, you will see that over the last one hundred years, what has been valued in leadership has constantly shifted, and many management fads have come and gone in that time. A hundred years ago, teams worked under command-and-control practitioners: leaders who proudly swore that they didn't get ulcers; they gave them. That later shifted to various management systems. Teams have functioned under management by fear, management by objectives, and participatory management. But in recent years there has been a shift back to some basics that draw on ancient wisdom: showing respect, developing trust, identifying vision, listening to people, reading the environment, and acting with courage.

In the sixth century BC, the Chinese sage Lao-Tzu advised leaders to be selfless and to keep egocentricity in check to become more effective. He encouraged them to lead without dominating, to be open and receptive. "The wise leader," he said, "is like a midwife, not intervening unnecessarily, so that when the child is born, the mother can rightly say, 'We did it ourselves!'" That kind of a mindset requires a more relational approach to leadership.

During the course of my career, I have changed from a climber to a connector, and I have no regrets. I can summarize the progress of my thinking in the following way:

I want to win.
I want to win, and you can too.
I want to win with you.
I want you to win, and I'll win too.

Success is fleeting—but relationships are lasting. If you take a connector's approach to leadership and put your team ahead of your own career advancement, you have a much better chance of succeeding because no one ever achieved anything of significance working alone. Besides, even if you don't succeed in a given endeavor, you will have at least built some relationships and made some friends along the way. That not only makes the journey more pleasant, but it sets you up for success in the future. You never know how you and your team members might be able to help one another in the future as you strive onward in leadership.

THE SELF-AWARE LEADER'S
QUESTIONS FOR REFLECTION

In what ways am I putting myself and my career ahead of the people on my team? What action can I take to better serve my people and put them ahead of my personal agenda?

_____

_____

_____

_____

_____

_____

_____

_____

_____

_____

_____

_____

FOUR

LOOK AT YOURSELF
WHEN PEOPLE QUIT

....

For many years, I taught multi-day leadership conferences. One of the things I enjoyed most about doing them was my time interacting with people and doing Q and A sessions. One of the comments heard often was, "I love your leadership principles, and your ideas are good, but you have no idea how bad a leader I work for. What do I do?" As a result of those remarks, I ended up writing a book titled *How to Lead When Your Boss Can't (or Won't).*

One day as an attendee was talking about how difficult it was to work for his leader, I took an informal poll. I asked, "How many of you have ever worked for a bad leader?" The response was overwhelming. An audible groan rose from the audience and nearly every person raised a hand. With a flash of insight, I asked, "How many have ever quit a job because of a bad leader at work?" Again, almost every person raised a hand. And it confirmed what I already believed to be true: when people quit their jobs, the leaders need to look at themselves to see if they are the reason.

THE DOOR SWINGS BOTH WAYS

All organizations have an influx and outflow of employees that looks similar to people entering and leaving through a revolving door. People come in through the door because they have a reason to be part of that company. Perhaps the vision of the organization resonates with them. Or they believe the company holds great opportunities for them. Or they value the benefits the company offers. Or they simply need to earn money. There are almost as many reasons as there are people who apply.

But when people exit the company through that same door, chances are high that most of them have something in common. Their desire to leave for "greener pastures" is often motivated by the need to get away from a poor leader.

It has been my privilege to lead non-profit organizations, for-profit companies, and volunteer organizations. People come and go in every type of organization, but they *go* away fastest from a poorly led volunteer organization. People in those organizations have no paycheck to keep them. When their leaders are bad, they simply leave. If there are a lot of bad leaders, a flood of people keeps that revolving door spinning as they depart looking for another organization to join.

WHO PEOPLE QUIT

As leaders, we'd like to think that when people leave our team or organization, it has little to do with us. But the reality is that we are often the reason. Some sources estimate that as many as sixty-five percent of people leaving companies do so because of their managers. We may say that people quit their job or their company, but the reality is that they usually quit their leaders. The "company" doesn't do anything negative to them. People do. Sometimes coworkers cause the problems that prompt people to leave. But often the people who alienate employees are their direct supervisors.

Most leaders can make a good impression on employees when they first meet. Add to that the optimism people have when they start a new job. Everyone wants a new job to work out. But over time, people recognize leaders for who they really are, not who they are trying to appear to be. If a boss is a jerk, it's only a matter of time before employees know it.

So what kind of leaders do employees quit? Most often they come in four types:

1. People Quit Leaders Who Devalue Them

An elderly couple, George and Mary Lou, were celebrating their golden wedding anniversary. With the divorce rate so high, a reporter wondered about their secret for success. So he asked George, "What is your recipe for a long, happy marriage?"

George explained that after their wedding, his new father-in-law took him aside and handed him a little package. Inside the package was a gold watch that George still used. He showed it to the reporter. Across the face of the watch, where he could see it a dozen times a day, were written the words, "Say something nice to Mary Lou."

All of us like to hear good things said about us and to us. We all want to be appreciated. However, many people don't receive positive feedback or appreciation from their leaders at work. Often it is quite the opposite; they feel devalued. Their bosses act superior and treat them with disdain or, worse, contempt. And that spells disaster for any relationship—even a professional working relationship.

Malcolm Gladwell, in his book *Blink*, writes about a relationship expert named John Gottman who was reliably able to predict the potential success of a couple's marriage based on their interaction with one another. What was it that indicated that a marriage relationship was headed for disaster? Contempt. If one of the partners treated the other with contempt, the relationship was usually doomed to fail.[1]

> It is impossible to add value to someone we devalue!

It is impossible to add value to someone we devalue! If we don't respect someone, we cannot treat them with respect. Why? We cannot consistently behave in a way that is inconsistent with our beliefs.

It has been my observation that when leaders devalue people on their team, they begin to manipulate them. They start treating them like objects, not people. That is never appropriate for a leader to do.

So what is the solution? Look for people's value and express your appreciation for them. Leaders are often good at finding value in an opportunity or a deal. They need to have a similar mindset when it comes to the people on their team.

Find the value in the people who work for you. Praise them for their contribution. They may contribute value to customers with the products they produce or the services they provide. They may contribute value to the organization by increasing its overall worth. They may contribute value to their coworkers, building them up or maximizing their performance. Find something to appreciate, share it with them, and they will appreciate working for you.

2. People Quit Leaders Who Are Untrustworthy

Michael Winston, former managing director and chief leadership officer for Countrywide Financial Corporation (which is now part of Bank of America Corp.), said:

> Effective leaders ensure that people feel strong and capable. In every major survey on practices of effective leaders, trust in the leader is essential if other people are going to follow that person over time. People must experience the leader as believable, credible, and trustworthy. One of the ways trust is developed—whether in the leader or any other person—is through consistency in behavior. Trust is also established when words and deeds are congruent.

Have you ever worked with people you couldn't trust? It's a terrible experience. Nobody likes to work with someone they can't rely on. A survey conducted by Manchester Consulting in Philadelphia indicated that trust in the workplace is unfortunately on the decline. They discovered that the five quickest ways that leaders lost the trust of their people in the workplace were:

- Acting inconsistently in what they say and do
- Seeking personal gain above shared gain
- Withholding information
- Lying or telling half-truths
- Being close-minded

When leaders break trust with their people, it is like the breaking of a mirror. And while it may be possible to recover all of the pieces and glue them back together, the mirror will always show cracks. The greater the damage done, the more distorted the image is. It becomes very difficult to overcome the damage done in a relationship when trust has been broken.

In contrast, the survey found that the best ways for leaders to *build* trust were to:

- Maintain integrity
- Openly communicate their vision and values
- Show respect for fellow employees as equal partners

- Focus on shared goals more than their personal agendas
- Do the right thing regardless of personal risk[2]

Building and maintaining trust as a leader is a matter of integrity and communication. If you don't want people to quit you as a leader, you need to be consistent, open, and truthful with them.

3. People Quit Leaders Who Are Incompetent

As I mentioned at the beginning of this chapter, one of the complaints I hear most often from people is that they work for a bad leader. They often go on to say that their leader is bad at more than leadership. Everyone wants to feel that their leaders are capable of doing their jobs in their field, whether they are a worker on the factory floor, a salesperson, a mid-level manager, an athlete, or a volunteer. Leaders need to inspire confidence, and they do that, not with charisma, but with competence.

When leaders are incompetent, they become a distraction to the team. They waste people's energy. They prevent people from keeping the main thing the main thing. They take the focus from the vision and values of the organization and place it on their own behavior. If the people working for an incompetent leader have a high degree of skill, they will continually worry about the leader messing things up, causing them to expend time and energy fixing messes. If people lack skill or experience, they won't know what to do to fix things. No matter what, productivity declines, morale suffers, and positive momentum becomes impossible.

> Leaders need to inspire confidence, and they do that, not with charisma, but with competence.

An incompetent leader will not lead competent people for long. The Law of Respect in *The 21 Irrefutable Laws of Leadership* states, "People naturally follow leaders stronger than themselves." People whose leadership ability is a 7 (on a scale of 1 to 10) won't follow a leader who is a 4. Instead, they quit and find someone else— somewhere else—to lead them.

That means you continually need to develop your leadership skills and professional abilities. If you're not, at some point you won't be able to help your people effectively.

4. People Quit Leaders Who Are Insecure

If a leader values people, possesses integrity, and displays competence, then people will be content to follow, right? Not necessarily. Even if leaders possess those three qualities, there is still one characteristic that will drive people away from them: insecurity.

Some insecure leaders are easy to spot. Their desire for power, position, and recognition comes out in an obvious display of fear, suspicion, distrust, or jealousy. But sometimes it can be more subtle. Exceptional leaders do two things: they develop other leaders, and they work themselves out of a job. Insecure leaders never do that. Instead, they try to make themselves indispensable. They don't want to train their people to reach their potential because they don't want people on their team to be more successful than they are. In fact, they don't want them to be able to succeed without their help. And anytime someone who works for them rises up to too high a level, insecure leaders see it as a threat.

People want to work for leaders who fire them up, not those who put out their fire. They want leaders who will lift them up and help them fly, not tie them down. They want mentors who will help them reach their potential and succeed. If they perceive that their leader is more concerned with maintaining their authority and protecting their position, they will eventually find someone else to work for.

RECIPE FOR RETENTION

No matter how good a leader you are, you will occasionally lose people. That's simply a part of leadership.

However, you can do things to make yourself the kind of leader that other people want to follow. Here are the things I do when people quit, to look at myself to see if I'm the problem.

1. I take responsibility for my relationships with others. When a relationship goes bad, I initiate action to try to make the relationship better. Even if that doesn't make them decide to stay, it's the right thing to do. If you want to be a better leader, you need to do that too.

2. When people leave me, I do an exit interview. Why guess the reason someone is leaving when you can ask them? The purpose of an exit interview is to discover if I am the reason they are leaving. If I do, I apologize and take the high road with them.

3. I put a high value on those who work with me. It's wonderful when the people believe in their leader. It's more wonderful when the leader believes in the people. If my people are leaving because I'm making them feel devalued, I want to know, so I can make a change.

4. I put credibility at the top of my leadership list. I may not always be competent; there are times when every leader finds himself in over his head. However, I can always be trustworthy. I choose to be honest no matter the circumstances. That's a choice you can make too.

5. I recognize that my positive emotional health creates a secure environment for people. When the leader is secure and positive, the people are free to be at their best. Therefore, I choose to think positively, practice right behavior toward others, and follow the golden rule.

6. I will have a teachable spirit and nurture my passion for personal growth. My leadership future and my people's progress are dependent on my getting better. Therefore, I keep learning so I can continue leading. If I keep growing, I will never become the "lid" on the potential of my people.

> It's wonderful when the people believe in their leader. It's more wonderful when the leader believes in the people.

One of the worst things that can happen to an organization is to lose its best people. When that happens, don't blame it on the company, the competition, the market, or the economy. Blame it on leadership. People quit people, not companies. If you want to keep your best people and help your organization fulfill its mission, then become a better leader.

THE SELF-AWARE LEADER'S
QUESTIONS FOR REFLECTION

Have I driven away good people by being a poor leader? How can I change to become more positive, uplifting, trustworthy, competent, and secure?

_____

_____

_____

_____

_____

_____

_____

_____

_____

_____

_____

_____

FIVE

LISTEN MORE THAN TALK

....

Steven B. Sample, in his book *The Contrarian's Guide to Leadership*, writes, "The average person suffers from three delusions: (1) that he is a good driver, (2) that he has a good sense of humor, and (3) that he is a good listener." I don't know about you, but I plead guilty on all three counts! And the place where I know I need the most help is as a listener.

I will never forget the time a woman I worked with confronted me about my poor listening skills. She said, "John, when people talk to you, often you seem distracted and look around the room. We're not sure that you are listening to us!"

I was surprised because, like most people, I *really did* think I was a good listener. The first thing I did was apologize. I trusted the opinion of the person who had confronted me, and I knew it had taken courage for her to tell me, because I was her boss. The second thing I did was start trying to change. For several years I made it a regular practice to put an "L" in the corner of my legal pad anytime I was in a meeting to remind myself to *listen*. Sometimes I would write "LL" to remind myself to *look* at them while I listened. It made a big difference in my leadership.

Sample also says, "Many leaders are terrible listeners; they actually think talking is more important than listening. But contrarian leaders know it is better to listen first and talk later. And when they listen, they do so artfully."

The positive benefits of being a good listener are much more valuable than we often recognize. I once read a humorous story that Jim Lange included in his book *Bleedership*.

> A couple of country boys are out in the woods hunting when one of them falls to the ground. He doesn't seem to be breathing and his eyes are rolled back in his head.
>
> The other guy whips out his cell phone and calls 911.

He frantically tells the operator, "Bubba is dead! What can I do?"

The operator, in a calm, soothing voice says, "Just take it easy. I can help. First, let's make sure he's dead."

There is silence, and then a shot is heard.

The guy's voice comes back on the line and says, "Okay, now what?"

As this story illustrates—we can hear what is said without really listening to what is being communicated. The hunter above heard what the operator told him and technically did make sure that his hunting companion was dead. But had he really been listening, I don't think he would have shot his partner.[1]

The story may seem silly, but it contains an important truth. When we hear without really listening, our leadership is bound to suffer—and so will our followers. That's why my advice to leaders is to listen, learn, and then lead.

I once read about a study that stated that we hear half of what is being said, listen to half of what we hear, understand half of that, believe half of that, and remember only half of that. If you translate those assumptions into an eight-hour workday, here is what it would mean:

You spend half your day—about four hours—in
    listening activities.
You hear about two hours' worth of what is said.
You actually listen to an hour of it.
You understand only thirty minutes of that hour.
You believe only fifteen minutes' worth.
And you remember less than eight minutes of all
    that is said.

That's a pretty poor average track record. And it
shows that we all need to work much harder at actively
listening!

WHY LISTENERS ARE MORE EFFECTIVE
LEADERS THAN TALKERS

Because of my desire to be a more effective listener, I
have actively observed leaders for years and paid close
attention to how the effective ones listen to others. And
I have come to some conclusions about the impact of
good listening related to leadership:

1. Understanding People Precedes Leading Them

Leadership finds its source in understanding. To
be worthy of the responsibility of leadership, a person
must have insight into the human heart. Sensitivity

toward the hopes and dreams of people on your team is essential to connecting with them and motivating them.

In my book *The 21 Irrefutable Laws of Leadership*, I write about the Law of Connection, which states, "Leaders touch a heart before they ask for a hand." Not only is it not fair to ask for the help of someone with whom you haven't connected, it is also ineffective. And you cannot connect with someone if you don't understand them. If you want to be more effective connecting with people, make it your goal to understand them. It will make you a better leader.

> Leadership finds its source in understanding.

2. Listening Is the Best Way to Learn

It is no accident that we have one mouth and two ears. When we fail to listen, we shut off much of our learning potential. You've probably heard the phrase "seeing is believing." Well, so is listening. Talk show host Larry King said, "I remind myself every morning: nothing I say this day will teach me anything. So, if I'm going to learn, I must do it by listening."

In 1997 I moved to Atlanta, Georgia. Immediately I realized the influence of the African American community upon the city. I wanted to connect with people in that community and learn about their journey. I asked my friend Sam Chand to set up four lunches with some top African-American leaders. For me, it was one of the greatest learning experiences of my life. Our time together was filled with our getting acquainted, my asking questions, and my listening to wonderful stories. I left each lunch with new friends and greater respect for the people I met and for their life experiences.

In 2020 as people gathered around the U.S. and protested the shooting of unarmed Black people, I again turned to Black friends in the community to help me understand their perspective on racism and the problems we're facing as a nation. I asked questions and listened so that I could learn.

3. Listening Can Keep Problems from Escalating

A Cherokee proverb says, "Listen to the whispers and you won't have to hear the screams." Good leaders are attentive to small issues. They pay attention to their intuition about whispers. And they pay close attention to what *isn't* being said. That requires more than just good listening skills. It starts with a good understanding of people, and it also means being secure enough to ask for honest communication from others and not to become defensive when receiving it. To be an effective leader, you need to let others tell you what you *need* to hear, not necessarily what you *want* to hear.

Gordon Bethune, former CEO of Continental

> "Listen to the whispers and you won't have to hear the screams."
> —CHEROKEE PROVERB

Airlines, took this idea a step further when he advised, "Make sure you only hire people who will be willing to kick the door open if you lose direction and close it. You may be able to ignore somebody's opinion if you don't like it, but if the person has the data to back it up, your intellect should be able to overwhelm your vanity."[2]

A common fault that occurs in people as they gain more authority is impatience with those who work for them. Leaders like results. Unfortunately, that action orientation sometimes causes them to stop listening. But a deaf ear is the first symptom of a closed mind, and having a closed mind is a surefire way to hurt your leadership.

The higher people go in leadership, the more authority they wield, and the less they are *forced* to listen to others. However, their *need* to listen becomes greater than ever! The further leaders get from the front lines, the more they must depend on others for accurate information. As you advance in leadership, if you haven't formed the habit of listening—carefully and intelligently—you aren't going to get the information you need. And when a leader stays in the dark, whatever problems the organization is having will only get worse.

4. Listening Establishes Trust

Effective leaders are always good communicators, but that means much more than just being a good talker. David Burns, a medical doctor and adjunct clinical professor emeritus in the Department of Psychiatry and Behavioral Sciences at the Stanford University School of Medicine, points out, "The biggest mistake you can make in trying to talk convincingly is to put your highest priority on expressing your ideas and feelings. What most people really want is to be listened to, respected, and understood. The moment people see that they are being understood, they become more motivated to understand your point of view."

Author and speaker Brian Tracy says, "Listening builds trust, the foundation of all lasting relationships." Those years ago when my employee confronted me about my poor listening skills, what she was really telling me was that I was not trustworthy. She didn't know whether her ideas, opinions, and feelings were safe with me. By becoming a more attentive listener, I was able to earn her trust.

> "Listening builds trust, the foundation of all lasting relationships."
> —BRIAN TRACY

When leaders listen to followers and use what they hear to make improvements that benefit those who speak up and the organization, then followers put their trust in those leaders. When leaders do the opposite—when they fail to listen—it damages the leader-follower relationship. When team members no longer believe that their leaders are listening to them, they start looking for someone who will.

5. Listening Can Improve the Organization

The bottom line is that when leaders listen, the organization gets better. Former Chrysler chairman Lee Iacocca asserted, "Listening can make the difference between a mediocre company and a great one." That means listening to people up and down the line at every level of the organization—to customers, workers, and other leaders.

Dallas-based Chili's, one of the nation's top restaurant chains, has prided itself in having leaders who listen. The late Norman Brinker, onetime owner and chairman of Chili's, believed that responsive communication is the key to good relations with employees and customers. He also learned that such communication pays big dividends. Almost eighty percent of the Chili's menu has come from suggestions made by unit managers.

Listening always pays dividends. The more you know, the better off you are—as long as you maintain perspective and think like a leader. Nicolo Machiavelli, author of *The Prince*, wrote, "Minds are of three kinds. One is capable of thinking for itself; another is able to understand the thinking of others; and a third can neither think for itself nor understand the thinking of others. The first is of the highest excellence, the second is excellent, and the third is worthless." To be a good leader, you must be able not only to think for yourself but also understand and learn from the thinking of others.

Is it possible to be a leader without being a listener? The answer is yes. Talk to employees in companies all across the country, and they will tell you that they work for people who do not listen to them. Is it possible to be a *good* leader, a self-aware leader, without listening? The answer is no. No one can go to the highest level and take their organization there without being a good listener. It is unlikely to happen, because you can never get the best out of people if you don't know who they are, where they want to go, why they care, how they think, and what they have to contribute. You can learn those things only if you listen.

> "One of the greatest gifts you can give anyone is the gift of attention."
> —JIM ROHN

Author and speaker Jim Rohn says, "One of the greatest gifts you can give anyone is the gift of attention." I believe that's true. But listening to followers isn't just a gift to them. It benefits the leader too. When leaders listen, they receive others' insight, knowledge, wisdom, and respect. That puts all of an organization's

assets into play, ready to be marshaled for the fulfill-
ment of the vision and the attainment of its goals. What
a wonderful gift.

THE SELF-AWARE LEADER'S
QUESTIONS FOR REFLECTION

Do I spend more time talking or listening to my team members?
Why? What would happen if I spent more time asking questions
and listening? How can I start doing that beginning today?

_____

_____

_____

_____

_____

_____

_____

_____

_____

SIX

HANDLE CRITICISM
WITH GRACE

....

One of the prices of leadership is receiving criticism. Leadership means going first, standing out, taking risks, trying to take ground. Others notice you, and not everyone will agree with how you lead.

As a young leader I liked leading. I liked being out front and being noticed. I enjoyed the praise of the people. However, I didn't want to put up with anybody's "constructive criticism." Very quickly I learned that I had unrealistic expectations. No leader, no matter how good, gets only praise (and I certainly wasn't good when I got started). If you want to be a leader, you need to get used to criticism, because whether you fail or succeed, you *will* be criticized. Some of the criticism will be deserved. If you receive it with grace and learn from it, you will benefit. Other criticism will be unfair. Some people will always find something to be unhappy about, and the way they criticize others, you'd think they got paid for it! But you need to respond well to that kind of criticism too.

Being criticized can be very discouraging. One day when I was feeling down, I shared my weariness with criticism to a friend, and his response was enlightening.

"When you're getting discouraged as a leader," he said, "think of Moses. He led a million complaining people for forty years and never arrived where he was supposed to go." Moses faced a lot of complaints, criticism, and just plain whining. Some days as a leader, I can sympathize with Moses. I bet if he had it to do all over again, he would have made a note to self: next time don't tell Pharaoh to let *all* my people go.

HOW DO YOU HANDLE CRITICISM?

I love the story of the salesman who was getting a haircut and mentioned that he was about to take a trip to Rome, Italy. He expected his barber to be excited because he was Italian.

"Rome is a terribly overrated city," commented his barber, who was born in northern Italy. "What airline are you taking?"

The salesman told him the name of the airline and the barber responded, "What a terrible airline! Their seats are cramped, their food is bad, and their planes are always late. What hotel are you staying at?"

The salesman named the hotel, and the barber exclaimed, "Why would you stay there? That hotel is in the wrong part of town and has horrible service. You'd be better off staying home!"

"But I expect to close a big deal while I'm there," the salesman replied. "And afterward I hope to see the pope."

"You'll be disappointed trying to do business in Italy," said the barber. "And don't count on seeing the pope. He only grants audiences to very important people."

Three weeks later the salesman returned to the barber shop. "And how was your trip?" asked the barber.

"Wonderful!" replied the salesman. "The flight was perfect, the service at the hotel was excellent, and I made a big sale. And," the salesman paused for effect, "I got to meet the pope!"

"You got to meet the pope?" Finally, the barber was impressed. "Tell me what happened!"

"Well, when I approached him, I bent down and kissed his ring."

"No kidding! And what did he say?"

"He looked down at my head and said, 'My son, where did you ever get such a lousy haircut?'"

Not everyone handles criticism the same way. Some try to ignore it. Some try to defend themselves against it. Others, like the salesman, use a witty remark to put a critic in his place. But no matter what, if you are a leader, you *will* have to deal with criticism. And if you can do it with grace, people will respect you.

HOW TO HANDLE CRITICISM WITH GRACE

Since all leaders have to deal with negativity and criticism, regardless of position or profession, it's important for them to learn to handle it constructively. Greek philosopher Aristotle said, "Criticism is something you can avoid easily—by saying nothing, doing nothing, and being nothing." However, that isn't an option for anyone who wants to be successful as a leader. So what do you do? The following four-step process has helped me deal with criticism, so I pass it on to you.

> "Criticism is something you can avoid easily—by saying nothing, doing nothing, and being nothing."
> —ARISTOTLE

1. Know Yourself—This Is a Reality Issue

As a young leader, it took only a year for me to discover that anyone having an up-front position was certain to draw criticism. Some environments are like the office in which the following sign is said to have been displayed:

> **NOTICE:**
> This department requires no physical fitness program: everyone gets enough exercise jumping to conclusions, flying off the handle, running down the boss, knifing friends in the back, dodging responsibility, and pushing their luck.
> **—Anonymous**

Since you know you will be criticized as a leader, what should you do? First, have a realistic view of yourself. That will lay a solid foundation for you to handle criticism successfully. Self-awareness is your friend. Here's why. When a leader is being criticized, it's often really the leadership position that prompts the negative remarks, not the individual leader. You need to be able to separate the two, and you can do that only when you know yourself. If a criticism is directed at the position, it's not personal. You should let it roll off of you. Knowing yourself well may take some time and effort.

As Founding Father Benjamin Franklin observed, "There are three things extremely hard: steel, a diamond, and to know one's self." However, the effort is worth the reward.

I have to admit that the majority of criticism I have received over the years has been directed more at me than at the position I held. The good news is that it often helped me know myself better. I soon learned that when others began the conversation with the phrase, "I'm going to tell you something for your own good," they rarely seemed to have anything good to tell me! However, I also realized that what I need to hear most is usually what I want to hear least. From those conversations I have learned much about myself, including the following:

- I am impatient.
- I am unrealistic about the time things take and how difficult the process is.
- I don't like to spend a lot of time on people's emotional issues.
- I overestimate the ability of others.
- I assume too much.
- I want to delegate responsibility too quickly.
- I want options—so many that I can drive people crazy.
- I don't care for rules or restrictions.
- I determine my priorities quickly and expect others to do the same.

- I process issues quickly and want to move on—
  even when other people aren't ready.

Obviously, the things I have found out about myself are not flattering. Yet those weaknesses are a reality. Self-awareness is about identifying both weaknesses and strengths. So the question is, "What am I to do?"

2. Change Yourself—This Is a Responsibility Issue

Author Aldous Huxley remarked, "You shall know the truth and the truth shall make you mad." To be more self-aware as a leader, I need to examine criticism objectively, no matter how it's delivered. My first natural reaction to criticism often isn't good—it's sometimes hurt feelings, but more often it's anger. But after my anger has subsided, my first step is to determine whether the criticism itself is constructive or destructive. (Some say constructive criticism is when I criticize you, but destructive criticism is when you criticize me!) Here are the questions I ask to get to determine what kind of criticism it is:

> "You shall know the truth and the truth shall make you mad."
> —ALDOUS HUXLEY

- **Who criticized me?** Adverse criticism from a wise person is more to be desired than the enthusiastic approval of a fool. The source often matters.

71

- **How was it given?** I try to discern whether the person was being hostile or judgmental, or whether he gave me the benefit of the doubt and spoke with kindness.
- **Why was it given?** Was it given out of a personal hurt or for my benefit? Hurting people hurt people; they lash out or criticize to try to make themselves feel better, not to help the other person. But criticism can also come because people are genuinely trying to help.

Constructive criticism is always easier to accept. But even destructive criticism needs to be mined for truth. And when I determine that someone's criticism about me is accurate, then I have a responsibility to do something to address it. That is part of becoming a better leader. If I respond correctly to my critics by examining myself and admitting my shortcomings, then I set myself up to begin making positive changes in my life. If I defend myself and deny my weaknesses, I decrease my self-awareness and stop my growth as a leader.

Whether the criticism is legitimate or not, what determines my growth as a leader is my attitude toward receiving it. My friend, management expert Ken Blanchard, is right when he says when something goes wrong, some leaders are like seagulls: "Seagull managers fly in, make a lot of noise, dump on everyone, and then fly out."[1] People with that kind of attitude toward bad news not only refuse to take responsibility for their contribution to the problem, but they also make conditions worse for those people who work with them.

People can change for the better only when they are open to improvement, when they are willing to receive criticism with grace. For that reason, whenever I am criticized, I try to maintain the right attitude by:

Not being defensive,
Looking for the grain of truth,
Making the necessary changes, and
Taking the high road.

If I do those things, there is a very good chance that I will learn things about myself, improve as a leader, and preserve the relationships I have with others, including the members of my team.

3. Accept Yourself—This Is a Maturity Issue

Jonas Salk, developer of the Salk polio vaccine, had many critics in spite of his incredible contribution to medicine. Of criticism, he observed, "First people will tell you that you are wrong. Then they will tell you that you are right, but what you're doing really isn't important. Finally, they will admit that you are right and that

73

what you are doing is very important; but after all, they knew it all the time." How can leaders best handle this kind of confusing response from others? Learn to accept themselves. If you have endeavored to know yourself, and have worked hard to change yourself, then what more can you do?

Professor and author Leo Buscaglia counseled, "The easiest thing to be in the world is you. The most difficult thing to be is what other people want you to be. Don't let them put you in that position." To be the best person you can be—and the best leader—you need to be yourself. That doesn't mean that you aren't willing to grow and change. It just means that you work to become the best *you* that you can be. And as psychologist Carl Rogers remarked, "The curious paradox is that when I accept myself just as I am, then I can change." Being who you really are is the first step in becoming better than you are.

> Being who you really are is the first step in becoming better than you are.

Because I've already written about working within your strengths, which you can do only if you know and accept who you are, I don't need to say a lot more about it here, other than to emphasize that accepting yourself is a sign of maturity. If you worry too much about what other people think of you, it's because you have more confidence in their opinion than you have in your own. Or you're trying to hide who you really are. But if you know and admit your weaknesses, and you know your strengths and work within them, you can be yourself with confidence. And as executive coach and consultant Judith Bardwick says, "Real confidence comes from knowing and accepting yourself—your strengths and limitations—in contrast to depending on affirmation from others."

4. Forget Yourself—This Is a Security Issue

The final step in the process of effectively handling criticism is to stop focusing on yourself. When we were growing up, a lot of us spent a good deal of time worrying about how the world saw us. Now that I'm over seventy, I realize the world really was never paying much attention.

Secure people forget about themselves so they can focus on others. By doing this, they can face nearly any kind of criticism—and even serve the critics. For years I have gone out of my way to initiate personal contact with my critics. I seek them out and greet them. I want them to know that I value them as people, regardless of what their attitude is toward me. Being secure in who I am and focusing on others instead of myself allows me to take the high road with people. I try to live out a sentiment expressed by Pakenham Beatty, who advised,

"By your own soul learn to live. And if men thwart you, take no heed. If men hate you, have no care: Sing your song, dream your dream, hope your hope and pray your prayer."

As leaders, we must always be serious about our responsibilities, but it isn't healthy for us to take ourselves too seriously. A Chinese proverb says, "Blessed are those who can laugh at themselves. They shall never cease to be entertained." I must say, for years I have entertained myself.

My friend Joyce Meyer observes, "God will help you be all you can be, but he will never let you be successful at becoming someone else." We can't do more than try to be all that we can be. If we do that as leaders, we will give others our best, and we will sometimes take hits from others. But that's okay. That is the price for a leader. If we learn to take those hits with grace, take the high road, and keep leading, we will earn others' respect. And we will respect ourselves.

> "Blessed are those who can laugh at themselves. They shall never cease to be entertained."
> —CHINESE PROVERB

THE SELF-AWARE LEADER'S
QUESTION FOR REFLECTION

Where am I defending myself and pretending I have it all together when I should instead be gracefully accepting criticism and striving to improve?

_____

_____

_____

_____

_____

_____

_____

_____

_____

_____

_____

_____

SEVEN

ADMIT YOUR MISTAKES AND LEARN FROM THEM

....

Once at a leadership conference where I was teaching, a young man came up to me during a break and said, "I'm going to start my own organization."

"Good for you," I replied.

"Yeah," he continued, "I want to build a business 'the right way.' That way I won't have to deal with any problems."

"You know," I said as he was turning to leave, "you're making the mistake of thinking you won't make any mistakes."

IGNORANCE ISN'T BLISS

When you're young and idealistic, you think you can lead better than many of the people who have led before you. I know that was true for me. When I got started in my career, I was positive, aggressive, optimistic—and totally naïve. I often led by assumption. By that I mean that in my youthful zeal, I usually took for granted that everything was fine. I didn't look for problems because I didn't expect to find any. The result? I got blindsided. Whenever that occurred, I was bewildered. *How could such a thing happen?* I would wonder.

After getting blindsided for the fourth or fifth time, in desperation I started asking experienced leaders for help. One of those leaders told me something that changed my leadership. He said, "John, the biggest mistake you can make is to not ask what mistakes you are making."

That piece of advice set my leadership journey on a new course. It was my introduction to realistic thinking—something I was not accustomed to embracing. As I examined myself, I learned some things:

- I gave little thought to what might go wrong.
- I assumed that the "right way" would be mistake-free.
- I did not acknowledge mistakes I made to myself or to others.

79

- I was not learning from my mistakes.
- I was not helping others by teaching lessons learned from my mistakes.

If I wanted to become a better leader, I would need to change. I would have to stop making the mistake of not asking what mistake I was making. I needed to become intentional in admitting my mistakes and learning from them.

RECIPE FOR SUCCESSFUL FAILURE

No one ever sized people up more accurately than the person who invented the pencil eraser. Everyone makes mistakes—large and small. To get maximum attention, make a big mistake. To cause maximum damage, fail to admit it! That will keep you from growing as a leader. When it comes to defining failure or success, it's not about the number of mistakes you make; it's the number of times you make the same mistake. If you want to learn to fail successfully and handle the mistakes you *do* make with maximum profit, then you need to do the following five things:

> To get maximum attention, make a big mistake. To cause maximum damage, fail to admit it!

1. Admit Your Mistakes Quickly

Once when I was speaking to several CEOs at a conference, I encouraged them to be open about their mistakes and weaknesses with the people they lead. The room became very tense, and I could tell that they were resistant to my advice.

During the next break as I was signing books, the leader of a company asked to see me privately. When I could take a break, we moved away from the others and he said, "I disagree with your suggestion that we should be open to others about our failures." Then he began to tell me how important it was to put up a strong front and be totally confident in front of your people.

I heard him out, but when he was finished, I said, "You are leading others with a wrong assumption."

"What is it?" he asked.

"You assume that your people don't know your weaknesses or that they don't see your mistakes," I responded. "Trust me, they do. When you admit your mistakes, it is not a surprise to them; it is a reassurance. They'll be able to look at each other and say, 'Whew! He knows. Now we don't have to keep pretending!'"

The first step toward anticipating mistakes and learning from the ones you do make is to take a realistic look at yourself and admit your weaknesses. You can't improve as a leader if you're too busy trying to pretend you're perfect.

Former U.S. Navy captain Michael Abrashoff writes in his book *It's Your Ship*, "Whenever I could not get the results I wanted, I swallowed my temper and turned inward to see if I was part of the problem. I asked myself three questions: Did I clearly articulate the goals? Did I give people enough time and resources to accomplish the task? Did I give them enough training? I discovered that 90 percent of the time, I was at least as much a part of the problem as my people were."[1] Admitting our failures and taking responsibility for them will allow us to go to the next step.

> When it comes to success, it's not the number of mistakes you make; it's the number of times you make the same mistake.

2. Accept Mistakes as the Price of Progress

Psychologist Joyce Brothers asserts, "The person interested in success has to learn to view failure as a healthy, inevitable part of the process of getting to the top." Nothing is perfect in this life—and that includes you! You'd better start getting used to it. If you want to move forward, you're going to make mistakes.

Pro Football Hall of Fame quarterback Joe Montana remarked, "As if screwing up on the field in front of millions of TV viewers wasn't enough, the

Monday after every game I got to relive my mistakes—over and over again, in slow motion and with commentary from the coaches! Even when we won, we always took time to review our mistakes. When you're forced to confront your mistakes that often, you learn not to take your failures so personally. I learned to fail fast, learn from my mistakes and move on. Why beat yourself up about it? Just do better next time."

> "The person interested in success has to learn to view failure as a healthy, inevitable part of the process of getting to the top."
> —JOYCE BROTHERS

Not everyone is willing to confront his mistakes and not take them personally. Because Montana did, he become one of the best players in the history of the NFL. His leadership and ability to handle adversity earned him the nickname "Joe Cool." Those qualities also helped him to win four Super Bowls and be named Super Bowl MVP three times. If you want to reach your potential as a leader, accept that mistakes are the price of progress.

3. Insist on Learning from Your Mistakes

Author and leadership expert Tom Peters writes, "From the smallest branch to the corporate level, there is nothing more useless than the person who says at the end of the day, as their own report card, 'Well, I made it through the end of the day without screwing up.'"

There are two common approaches people have to failure. While one person hesitates and avoids mistakes because he feels inferior, the other is busy making mistakes, learning from them, and becoming superior. People can either run from mistakes and hurt themselves, or learn from them and help themselves. People who try to avoid failure at all costs never learn and end up repeating the same mistakes over and over again. But those who are willing to learn from their failures never have to repeat them again. As author William Saroyan observed, "Good people are good because they have come to wisdom through failure. We get very little wisdom from success." People in leadership need to take their cue from scientists. In science, mistakes always precede the discovery of truth.

> "Good people are good because they have come to wisdom through failure. We get very little wisdom from success."
> —WILLIAM SAROYAN

4. Ask Yourself and Others, "What Are We Missing?"

Some people expect nothing but trouble. They are pessimistic, so they don't bother to look for anything good. Others, like me, have a natural tendency to assume that everything is good. But either of these kinds of thinking can hurt a leader. Elizabeth Elliot, author of *All That Was Ever Ours*, points out, "'All generalizations are false including this one,'[2] yet we keep making them. We create images—graven ones that can't be changed; we dismiss or accept people, products, programs and propaganda according to the labels they come under; we know a little about something, and we treat it like we know everything." Leaders need to be more discerning than that.

It is easy to make decisions based on what we know. But there are always things we don't know. It is easy to choose a direction based on what we see. But what about what we don't see? Reading between the lines is essential for good leadership. We are most likely to do this when we ask the question, "What are we missing?"

The value of asking, "What are we missing?" is that it causes everyone to stop and think. Many people can see what's obvious. It's much more difficult to determine what *isn't* there. Asking tough questions causes people to think differently. Not asking questions is to assume that a project is potentially perfect and that

> The value of asking, "What are we missing?" is that it causes everyone to stop and think.

if it's handled with care, there will be no problems. That simply isn't reality.

5. Give the People Around You Permission to Push Back

Recently I saw a sign in a high-pressure sales office that said, "Do you like to travel? Do you want to meet new friends? Do you want to free up your future? All this can be yours if you make one more mistake." Fear of making mistakes keeps many individuals from reaching their potential. Fear of being honest with leaders about the potential problems of a course of action has hurt many teams. The best leaders invite the opinions of the people on their teams.

When leaders don't get input from others on their team, it can lead to disaster. Abrashoff touches on this problem in *It's Your Ship*. He writes,

> The moment I heard about it [the tragic sinking of a Japanese fishing boat off Honolulu by the submarine USS Greeneville], I was reminded that, as is often the case with accidents, someone senses possible danger but doesn't necessarily speak up. As the Greeneville investigation unfolded, I read in a *New York Times* article that the submarine's crew "respected the commanding officer too much to question his judgment." If that's respect, then I want none

of it. You need to have people in your organization that can tap you on your shoulder and
say, "Is this the best way?" or "Slow down," or
"Think about this," or "Is what we are doing
worth killing or injuring somebody?"

History records countless incidents in
which ship captains or organization managers permitted a climate of intimidation to
pervade the workplace, silencing subordinates
whose warnings could have prevented disaster.
Even when the reluctance to speak up stems
from admiration for the commanding officer's
skill and experience, a climate to question
decisions must be created in order to foster
double-checking.[3]

Many good minds working together are always
better than one working alone. Because I've learned
that lesson, I've changed from someone who avoids
potentially bad news to someone who invites it. For
many years I've given permission to members of my
inner circle to ask me hard questions and give me their
opinion when they disagree with me. I don't ever want
to make a mistake and then hear a team member say,
"I thought that was going to be a bad decision." I want
people to tell me on the front end, not after the fact.
Pushback before a decision is made is never disloyalty.

However, questioning a decision after it's made is not what I consider to be good teamwork.

If you lead people, then you need to give them permission to ask hard questions and push back against your ideas. That permission *must* be given to others by the leader. Too often leaders would rather have followers who turn a blind eye instead of ones who speak with a blunt tongue. But if all is quiet when decisions are being considered, it probably won't be quiet after it plays out. English philosopher-statesman Sir Francis Bacon observed, "If a person will begin with certainties, he will end in doubts; but if he will be content to begin with doubts, he will end in certainties."

———

Making mistakes won't make you a bad leader. But failing to admit your mistakes will. Only if you look for mistakes, admit mistakes, learn from mistakes, and anticipate mistakes will you and your team improve.

THE SELF-AWARE LEADER'S
QUESTIONS FOR REFLECTION

What mistakes am I overlooking or failing to admit? What lessons am I missing as a result? If I've been reluctant to admit mistakes, why? How can I change to grow in this area?

_____

_____

_____

_____

_____

_____

_____

_____

_____

_____

_____

_____

EIGHT

STOP MICROMANAGING PEOPLE AND START MANAGING YOUR PRIORITIES

....

There is a real temptation for most leaders to insert themselves into everything their team members do to make sure everything goes well. This is especially true for any leader who has a perfectionistic streak. However, if you want to be a better leader, you need to learn what needs your attention and what doesn't. And when it comes to working with your team, you should never micromanage them. Self-aware leaders keep themselves from overstepping. Instead, they give people the training they need, step back, and inspire them to be their best. They follow the advice given by General George S. Patton: "Don't tell people how to do things; tell them what to do and let them surprise you with their results."

Early in my career, I was a hands-on leader, involving myself in every area of the organization. I had to learn how to prioritize what was important for me to do personally, and what to leave to others. My eureka moment came while in a college classroom, where I was taking a business-management course. The professor was teaching the Pareto Principle, also known as the 80/20 Principle.[1] As he described the principle and its impact, my eyes were opened. He explained that:

> 80 percent of traffic jams occurs on 20 percent of the roads.
> 80 percent of beer is consumed by 20 percent of drinkers.
> 80 percent of classroom participation comes from 20 percent of students.
> 80 percent of the time you wear 20 percent of your clothes.
> 80 percent of the profits comes from only 20 percent of the customers.
> 80 percent of company problems is generated by 20 percent of the employees.

80 percent of sales is generated by 20 percent of
the salespeople.
80 percent of all decisions can be made on
20 percent of the information.

What an eye-opener! I realized it meant that the
most productive twenty percent of my activities were
sixteen times more productive than the remaining eighty
percent. If I wanted to decrease the complexity of my
life and increase my productivity, then I needed to focus
on my top twenty percent. The rest needed to be done
by others, who more than likely would do those tasks as
well as or better than I would. That day in the classroom
I realized two things: (1) I was doing too many things,
and (2) the things I was doing were often the wrong
things. And that is a recipe for an ineffective life!

FINDING THE MAIN THING

I immediately began to reevaluate the way I was spending my time. I knew I needed to prioritize my schedule,
so I started to ask myself three questions:

- What gives me the greatest return?
- What is most rewarding?
- What is required of me?

My answers would be the key to where I would manage *myself.* For the things I delegated, I would ask team members to manage *themselves.*

I'm not saying it's always easy to answer those three questions. Early in a career, the easiest to answer is usually the one concerning requirements. You can find those answers in a job description if you have one. On the other hand, most people don't start getting a true sense of what gives the greatest return for their effort until they reach their thirties—sometimes even later in life. And what is most rewarding to a person often changes during different seasons of life.

As I worked, reflected, and grew, I slowly began discovering the answers to those three key questions. My guiding principle was that the purpose of my work was *results.* If I wanted to accomplish objectives and be productive, I needed to provide forethought, structure, systems, planning, intelligence, and honest purpose to all that I did. But I also knew that I needed to keep things simple.

I had read a study of thirty-nine midsized companies stating that the characteristic that differentiated the successful companies from the unsuccessful was simplicity. The companies that sold few products, to fewer customers, and who worked with fewer suppliers than other companies in the same industry, were more profitable. Simple, focused operations were more profitable. As Warren Buffet observes, "The business schools reward difficult, complex behavior more than simple behavior, but simple behavior is more effective." By striving for simplicity, I could help myself to remain focused on what I did best, giving that my best energy, and trusting others to do their best in the areas where they shone.

> "The business schools reward difficult complex behavior more than simple behavior, but simple behavior is more effective."
> —WARREN BUFFET

During this season of my life, I changed from a doer of many things to a leader of a few things. Key to this transition were five decisions I made that helped me become more focused and productive. They will help you as you work harder to manage yourself and resist the urge to micromanage others.

1. I Determined Not to Know Everything

Some people believe that great leaders have all the answers. Not true. Successful leaders don't know everything. But they know people who do. If you ask me a question related to one of my organizations and I don't know the answer, I know which person in the organization does. If you ask about my profession, I may not know the answer, but with a phone call or two, I can talk to someone who can answer the question. And if you ask about the details of my life and schedule and I don't know the answer, I guarantee you there's at least one person who does—my assistant.

The most important decision I ever made to keep me focused and to simplify my life was to hire a top-notch assistant. For more than thirty years, that role has been filled by Linda Eggers. Her value to me has been enormous.

My assistant is the primary hub of information for my life. Everything flows to and through her. I trust her to know everything so that I don't have to. More important, she has learned how to sift information and grasp the most critical details. Remember, only twenty percent of all the information you receive will give you eighty percent of what you need to make good decisions. When we communicate, Linda gives me the essential information I

> **For leaders, it's better to know the most important things than to know everything.**

need, which enables me to see what to do next, helps me to know why it is important, and empowers me to bring the appropriate resources to bear on the need at hand. For leaders, it's better to know the most important things than to know everything. That's a big step away from micromanaging others.

If you're a leader and you don't have a good assistant, you need to try to hire one. That is the first and most important hiring decision every executive needs to make. If you have the right person in place, you can keep your mind on the main thing while your assistant thinks about everything else.

If you don't have an assistant or can't afford one, then you need to think about the members of your team with whom you can share the load. Get to know them and give them tasks that play to their strengths. Then get out of their way and allow them to succeed, fail, learn, and grow. Remember that most tasks don't need to be done your way. What's important is that the work be done in a way that most benefits the organization.

2. I Determined Not to Know Everything First

Most people have a strong natural desire to be "in the know." That's why gossip websites and tabloids do so well. Leaders also have a strong desire to be "in the know" when it comes to their organizations. No leader likes to be blindsided. However, good leaders can't afford to be caught up in every little detail of the organization. If they are, they lose their perspective and their ability to lead. What's the solution? Deciding that it's okay not to be the first to know everything.

In any organization, the best and fastest way to solve problems is always to find solutions at the lowest level possible. If every problem must be shared with leaders first, then solutions become more complex and take forever. Besides, the people on the front lines are usually the ones who provide the best solutions, whether it's on the production line, the battle line, or the breadline.

My assistant knows just about everything that happens in my organizations before I do. So does my CEO. So do the vice presidents of the different divisions. I trust them to know what's going on. They keep me informed with important information. And if they ever need to tell me bad news, I don't "shoot the messenger." Taking out your frustrations on the people who bring you bad information quickly stops the flow of communication.

> **In any organization, problems should always be solved at the lowest level possible.**

3. I Determined to Let Someone Represent Me

Every leader has to learn to stop merely taking personal action to fulfill the vision and start enlisting and empowering others to take action. (People who don't learn this lesson never become effective leaders.) However, not all leaders take the next difficult step of allowing other people to stand in for them as their representative to others. Why? Because it requires an even deeper level of trust. If someone misrepresents you, doesn't follow through, or does something unethical in your name, it reflects on you personally and may tarnish your reputation.

The decision to let others represent you requires much time and consideration. Trust should not be given thoughtlessly. You must get to know the people in whom you place that trust, and they must keep earning it through seasons of proven performance. The more you invest in those people, the lower the risk and higher the potential return. Once you reach that level of trust with your people, you will be freed up even more to remain focused on the main things that really matter.

I am blessed to have several people in my life who do this. Linda Eggers, my assistant, represents me in meetings, schedules my calendar, and handles my finances and correspondence. When she talks to others on my behalf, she speaks with my authority. Charlie Wetzel, my writer, communicates with my voice and ideas through the books we've worked on together. Mark Cole, my CEO, speaks on my behalf not only within my organizations but to leaders and organizations around the world. These people and others helped me to become more comfortable with letting go and trusting others.

Several years ago, my trust in others went to a whole other level. When it was suggested that we create a coaching organization using my name, I gave it a lot of thought before giving my consent. It felt like a big risk letting more people use my name, but I realized that if I wanted to expand my influence and extend my legacy, I had to allow others to represent me more broadly. That's when we created the John Maxwell Team. During team-member training, I spend a lot of time talking with them about my values and how I want them to value people. But then once they're trained, I have to trust them to do the right thing.

How should you decide whether someone else can be your representative, even when the pressure is on and the stakes are high? First, you must know their heart well enough to trust their character. Second, you must have enough history with them so that they know your heart and mind. Third, you must believe in their competence. If they can do the job eighty percent as well as you would, then they're ready. Let them represent you.

4. I Determined to Stay with My Strengths and Not Work on My Weaknesses

Half of being smart is knowing what you are dumb at. Since I went into this in-depth in the chapter "Know and Work Within Your Strengths," I don't need to here. But let me encourage you with these words I read in the *Gallup Management Journal*:

The most revealing discovery [about the great leaders they studied] was that effective leaders have an acute sense of their own strengths and weaknesses. They *know who they are*—and who they are not. They don't try to be all things to all people. Their personalities and behaviors are indistinguishable between work and home. They are genuine. It is this absence of pretense that helps them connect to others so well.[2]

I always strive to stay with my strengths. Perhaps I have learned this lesson well because it is my natural bent to focus on a few things. I do not like to dabble. I want to do something with excellence using my full concentration, or I want to delegate it. I have to admit, I am not a well-rounded person and I only do a few things well. But the bottom line is that in my areas of strength, I give everything I have and try to perform with excellence.

5. I Determined to Take Charge of What Took My Time and Attention

The final major step I took was to start managing myself better by taking control of my calendar. This was not easy for me. I enjoy helping people, and for the first few years of my career, I tended to let other people set my agenda and fill my calendar. Then one day I realized that I couldn't fulfill my purpose if I was forever fulfilling everyone else's.

> **Half of being smart is knowing what you are dumb at.**

Every leader is busy. The question for every

leader is *not* "Will my calendar be full?" The question is *"Who* will fill my calendar?" If you don't take charge of your schedule, others will always be in charge of you.

If you operate the way I did, you will have to change the way you choose what you do. I started my career doing the things I was taught to do in college—whether they had value or not. Then I started to do the things other people wanted me to do. As I became more proactive and sought to be successful, I did the things I saw other leaders doing. Finally, I started doing the things that *I* should do—the things that gave the greatest return and rewards. And I started delegating everything else.

C. W. Ceran remarked, "Genius is the ability to reduce the complicated to the simple." Keeping yourself focused on doing your best instead of micromanaging others requires simplification. If you can simplify your life, you will become more focused, you will possess more energy, and you will experience less stress. Like every decision in life, simplification requires trade-offs. You can't do everything, and choosing to do one thing means choosing not to do something else. It means saying no, even to some things you want to

> The question for every leader is *not* "Will my calendar be full?" The question is *"Who* will fill my calendar?"

do. But think about the alternative. If you don't choose what trade-offs you make, someone else will choose them for you.

Once at a convention of coaches, former Green Bay Packers coach Vince Lombardi was asked about his offensive and defensive strategies for winning football games. Other coaches had just described their elaborate schemes. Lombardi, who was famous for beginning training camp each year by holding up a football and saying, "This is a football," responded, "I only have two strategies. My offensive strategy is simple: When we have the ball, we aim to knock the other team down! My defensive strategy is similar: When the other team has the ball, we aim to knock all of them down!"[3] That may sound too simple, but it really is the bottom line for winning games in the NFL. Lombardi empowered his players to do just that, and as a result, they won Super Bowls.

> "Genius is the ability to reduce the complicated to the simple."
> —C. W. CERAN

When times get tough or deadlines loom, don't clamp down on your people. Empower them. If you can become better at managing your own priorities and resist the urge to micromanage others, you will become more effective and so will your team. That will benefit you, them, and your organization.

THE SELF-AWARE LEADER'S QUESTIONS FOR REFLECTION

Under pressure, do I try to control others on my team? Or do I work to prioritize my own responsibilities so I can be at my best? Where could I empower others more?

_____

_____

_____

_____

_____

_____

_____

_____

_____

_____

_____

_____

NINE

BECOME THE BEST LEARNER IN THE ROOM

....

I was having breakfast at the Holiday Inn in Lancaster, Ohio, with Curt Kampmeier, a salesman I had just met, when he leaned forward and asked me a question that would change the way I lived and led.

"John, what is your plan for personal growth?"

I proceeded to tell him all the initiatives I'd started as a leader and how hard I was working. As I talked, I described lots of plans, but none for personal growth. I didn't even know that I needed one!

Prior to that meeting, I believed that working hard

was enough to help me to grow and reach my potential. Wasn't that the way it was supposed to happen? You work hard, you climb the ladder, and someday you "make it"?

My futile attempt to impress Curt was like a plane circling an airport, waiting for clearance to land. Round and round I went until I finally ran out of gas.

"You don't have a personal plan for growth, do you?"

"No," I finally admitted, "I guess I don't."

The next thing he said was life changing.

"You know, John, people don't grow automatically," Curt explained. "To grow, you have to be intentional."

That conversation took place in 1973, though it's as clear in my memory as if it had happened last week. It spurred me to action. I immediately adopted a plan for growth in my life. And I determined to become a lifelong learner.

Coming out of that experience, personal growth has become one of the major themes of my life. And for decades I've talked to people at conferences about the issue of personal growth, and I've offered several different plans that I knew could help people. Sometimes I've been criticized for that. I remember a person coming up to me on one occasion and saying, "I don't like your plan for personal growth."

"That's okay," I replied. "What's your plan?"

"I don't have one," he said.

"Well, I like mine better!"

I suspect he believed that the only reason I talked about my growth plan was to sell books. What he didn't know was that I started talking about having a personal growth plan long before I ever had a book or video to sell. I had learned that people don't reach their potential by accident. The secret to success can be found in our daily agenda. If we do something intentional to grow every day, we move closer to reaching our potential. If we don't, our potential slowly slips away over the course of our lifetime.

If you want to be a self-aware leader, you've got to be an intentional learner. If you want to become the best leader you can be, you need to become the best learner in the room.

HOW WILL YOU GROW?

As you seek to learn and grow as a leader, I want to give you some advice about how to approach the process. After more than four decades of dedicated, continual effort to learn and grow, I offer the following suggestions:

1. Invest in Yourself First

Most leaders want to grow their business or organization. But what is the one thing—more than any other—that will determine the growth of that organization? The growth of the people in the organization And what determines the people's growth? The growth of their leader! As leaders, our limitations put lids on the people we lead. As long as people are following you, they will be able to travel only as far as you do. If you're not growing, it's less likely they will be growing. And if they desire growth and you're limiting them, they will leave and go somewhere else where they *can* grow.

As a young leader, I spent a lot of money on books and conferences. My wife, Margaret, and I had to make trade-offs to do this because we were on a very limited income. We often delayed other important expenditures so that we could invest in ourselves. Though it was difficult, our early investments in growth have compounded over the years, and they have given me a great return by improving my leadership.

Investing in yourself first may look selfish to some of the people around you. They may even criticize you for it. But if they do, they don't really understand how growth works. When airline flight attendants explain emergency procedures, they tell passengers to put their own oxygen mask on first before putting masks on their children. Is that instruction selfish? Of course not! The children's safety and well-being are dependent upon their parent being able to help them. As a leader, you have responsibility to your people. They are depending on you! If you're in no shape to lead well, where does that leave them?

If you look around, you can see a pattern at work in every area of life. Employees get better after their supervisor does. Kids get better after their parents do. Students get better after their teachers do. Customers get better after the salespeople do. Likewise, followers get better after their leaders do. It is a universal principle. President Harry S. Truman said, "You cannot lead others until you first lead yourself." You can lead yourself at your best only if you invest in yourself first.

2. Be a *Continual* Learner

When a leader reaches a particular position or level of training, there is a temptation to rest or slack off. That is a dangerous place to be. Rick Warren, author of *The Purpose Driven Life,* says, "The moment you stop learning is the moment you stop leading." If you want to lead, you have to learn. If you want to *continue* to lead, you must *continue* to learn. This will guarantee that you will be hungry for ever greater accomplishments. And it will help you to maintain credibility with your followers.

One of the most influential people in the golf world for many years was Harvey Penick. The author of the bestselling *Harvey Penick's Little Red Book: Lessons and Teachings from a Lifetime of Golf* taught pro players such as Ben Crenshaw, Tom Kite, Kathy Wentworth, Sandra

Palmer, and Mickey Wright how to improve their games. When Crenshaw won the Masters Tournament in 1995, he broke down and cried afterward because Penick, his lifelong mentor, had recently passed away.

You may be surprised to learn that Penick was largely self-taught. For decades he carried around a little red book in which he jotted down notes and observations to help him improve his game. He was a continual learner. And every time he got better, so did the people he taught. Ironically, Penick never intended to publish his notes. He simply planned to hand the book down to his son. But people convinced him to publish all the lessons he had learned over the years. As a result, people are still learning from him and benefiting from his wisdom.

If you want to lead, you must learn. If you want to *continue* to lead, you must *continue* to learn.

In my book *Winning with People*, I write about the Learning Principle, which says, "Every Person We Meet Has Potential to Teach Us Something." Maintaining an attitude of teachability is essential for being a continual learner. Contrary to popular belief, the greatest obstacle to discovery isn't ignorance or lack of intelligence. It's the illusion of knowledge. One of the great dangers of life is believing that you have arrived. Leaders who lack self-awareness often mistakenly believe that. If that happens to you, you're done growing.

Self-aware leaders don't see learning or achievement as a fixed destination to head for, and having arrived, to settle into—completed and finished. Not once have I heard a continual learner describe looking forward to arriving at the end of life's challenges. They are always looking further ahead and continue to exhibit an excitement, a curiosity, or a sense of wonder. One of their most engaging characteristics is their infectious desire to keep moving into the future, generating new challenges, and believing there is more to learn and accomplish. They understand that you can't conquer the world by staying in a safe harbor.

> The greatest obstacle to discovery isn't ignorance or lack of intelligence. It's the illusion of knowledge.

What kind of attitude do you have when it comes to learning? I've observed that people fall into one of several categories. They live in one of three zones:

- **The Challenge Zone:** "I attempt to do what I haven't done before."
- **The Comfort Zone:** "I do what I already know I can do."
- **The Coasting Zone:** "I don't even do what I've done before."

Everyone starts out in the challenge zone. As babies, we have to learn to eat, talk, and walk. Then we go to school and keep learning. But there comes a time in every person's life when they no longer *have* to keep trying new things. This is a pivotal period. For some people it occurs pretty early in life. For others, it comes after they achieve some degree of success. That's when they decide which zone they will live in: the challenge zone, where they continue to try new things, explore— and sometimes fail; the comfort zone, where they no longer take risks; or the coasting zone, where they don't even try anymore.

Something shifts when a person chooses to leave the challenge zone and stop growing. As Phillips Brooks asserted, "Sad is the day for any man when he becomes absolutely satisfied with the life he is living, the thoughts that he is thinking and the deeds that he is doing; when there ceases to be forever beating at the doors of his soul a desire to do something larger which he seeks and knows he was meant and intended to do."

There is no substitute for continual learning. Over the years I have developed a highly disciplined growth regimen:

I **READ** daily to grow in my personal life.
I **LISTEN** daily to broaden my perspective.
I **THINK** daily to apply what I learn.
I **FILE** daily to preserve what I learn.

I try to embrace the advice of German philosopher Goethe, who said, "Never let a day pass without looking at some perfect work of art, hearing some great piece of music and reading, in part, some great book."

Adopting this kind of regimen required me to change my mindset. During the first few years I was in leadership, I enjoyed being "Mr. Answer Man"—the expert others could come to for answers, the smartest person in the room. After my conversation with Curt in 1973, I decided to become "Mr. Open Man"—someone with a teachable attitude who desired to grow every day. I made it my goal to become the best *learner* in the room. My desire is to keep growing and learning until the day I die, not only for my own benefit, but for the benefit of others. I can never afford to forget what President John F. Kennedy said: "Leadership and learning are indispensable of each other."

> "Leadership and learning are indispensable of each other."
> —JOHN F. KENNEDY

3. Create a Growth Environment for the People You Lead

Soon after I dedicated myself to being a growing person, I came to the realization that most working environments are not conducive to growth. I saw that many of my old friends did not want to keep growing.

In their minds, they had paid their dues by attending and graduating from college. As far as they were concerned, they knew enough. They were done. In many ways, they were like the little girl who thought that she had exhausted mathematics when she had learned the twelve times tables. When her grandfather said with a twinkle in his eye, "What's thirteen times thirteen?" she scoffed, "Don't be silly, Grandpa, there's no such thing."

The road to success is uphill all the way, and most people are not willing to pay the price. Many people would rather deal with old problems than find new solutions. And people who are satisfied with being average will try to pull down anyone around them who is working to rise above that standard. To be a lifelong learner, I had to get out of a stagnant environment and distance myself from people who had no desire to grow. I sought out places where growth was valued and people were growing. This helped me to change and grow—especially in the beginning of my journey.

If you are investing in yourself and have adopted the attitude of a continual learner, you may think you've done all you need to do in the area of personal growth. But as a leader, you have one more responsibility. You need to create a positive growth environment for the people you lead. If you don't, the people in your organization who want to grow will find it difficult to do so, and they may eventually seek out other opportunities.

Creating a growth environment begins with your modeling growth. When you're the best learner in the room, the members of your team feel secure in being learners themselves instead of experts. But there are other factors that can create a good environment for growth. In a good growth environment, team members can look around and say to themselves:

- Others are ahead of me.
- I am continually challenged.
- My focus is forward.
- The atmosphere is affirming.
- I am often out of my comfort zone.
- I wake up excited.
- Failure is not my enemy.
- Others around me are growing.
- People desire change.
- Growth is modeled and expected of me.

If you can create an environment that looks like this, not only will the people on your team grow and improve, but others with great potential will knock down your doors to become part of your team! It will transform your organization.

THE PEOPLE DIFFERENCE

If you have not been focused on learning and have fallen into either the comfort zone or the coasting zone, then you may need to look for help to change. The good news is that help is all around you. Walt Disney remarked, "I am a part of all that I have met." The secret to your growth can be found in the people who surround you. People's attitudes and actions rub off on one another.

My father loves to tell the story of the man who tried to enter his mule in the Kentucky Derby. He was immediately rejected and rebuked.

"Your mule has no chance of winning a race against thoroughbreds," the race organizers chided.

"I know," the man replied, "but I thought the associations would do him some good."

Being around people who are better than we are tends to motivate us to stretch and improve ourselves. That is not always comfortable, but it is always profitable. It's said that whenever the great poet Emerson saw the great essayist Thoreau they would ask each other: "What has become clearer to you since last we met?" Each wanted to know what the other was learning. Great people desire to bring out the greatness in others. Small people will try to put the same limits on you that they have put on themselves.

I have Curt to thank for helping me understand

the value of growth so early in my career. Within a year of my conversation with him, I could tell that I was learning, growing, and changing. And I am continuing to grow. I'm still reading. I'm still asking questions. I'm still making appointments to meet with people who can teach me.

It's said that the Tatar tribes of central Asia used to have a curse that they would use on their enemies. They didn't tell them to get lost or to drop dead. Instead they would say, "May you stay in one place forever." What a horrible thought!

THE SELF-AWARE LEADER'S
QUESTIONS FOR REFLECTION

When I'm meeting with my team or colleagues, is my desire to be the expert or to learn? How often do I simply listen? How often do I ask questions? How often do I admit I don't understand something so that I can learn? What do I need to do to change my attitude and become a learner?

_____

_____

_____

_____

_____

_____

_____

_____

_____

_____

_____

TEN

JUDGE YOUR LEADERSHIP BY THE SUCCESS OF YOUR TEAM

....

When I was in my late twenties, I attended a conference where Lee Roberson was a speaker. He made a statement during a session that inspired me and changed my life. Roberson said, "Everything rises and falls on leadership." By that he meant that leaders have the power to make things better or worse for the people who follow them. Wherever you have good leaders, the team gets better, the department or division gets better, the organization gets better. And wherever you have bad leaders, everyone around them has a tougher time being successful. Leadership makes every endeavor either better or worse.

The moment I heard that statement, I understood intuitively that it was true. That statement soon became my theme. It has been a major inspiration and motivation for me for over forty years. It has been the foundation of the *21 Irrefutable Laws of Leadership,* including the Law of the Lid, which states, "Leadership ability determines a person's level of effectiveness." And it has influenced how I see everything that happens around me.

THE LEADER IS RESPONSIBLE

The more you understand leadership, the more you see how leaders impact things around them. A few years after I heard Roberson speak, along with millions of other Americans, I watched Jimmy Carter and Ronald Reagan debate one another prior to the 1980 presidential election. Most people agreed that the debate turned on a question that Reagan asked the American people. He said:

Next Tuesday is Election Day. Next Tuesday all of you will go to the polls and stand there in the polling place and make a decision. I think when you make that decision it might be well

119

if you would ask yourself, "Are you better off than you were four years ago? Is it easier for you to go buy things in the store than it was four years ago? Is there more or less unemployment in the country than there was four years ago?" If you answer all those questions yes, why, then I think your choice is very obvious as to who you'll vote for. If you don't agree, if you don't think that this course that we've been on for the last four years is what you would like to see us follow for the next four, then I could suggest another choice that you have.[1]

Why would that question—"Are you better off than you were four years ago?"—have such an impact? Because people understood that *their* current condition was the result of *who* their leader was. They didn't like their condition, so they changed leaders. It's what got Reagan elected. And it's why I say that you should judge your leadership by the success of your team. As leadership expert Max De Pree says, "The signs of outstanding leadership appear primarily among the followers."

People often attribute the success of organizations

> **"The signs of outstanding leadership appear primarily among the followers."**
> **—MAX DE PREE**

and teams to many things: opportunities, the economy, personnel, teamwork, resources, timing, chemistry, luck. And while it's true that any of those things can come into play, the one thing all good organizations have in common is good leadership.

Have you noticed that whenever you go to a new doctor, you have to fill out forms and answer a bunch of questions? Although they may seem trivial or irrelevant, the most important questions are those dealing with your family history. Why? Because your physical health is greatly determined by your parents' physical health. If one of your parents has heart disease, diabetes, or cancer, there is a high likelihood that you will someday have it too. Your health has been passed down to you.

Leadership works in a similar way. When leaders are healthy, the people they lead tend to be healthy. When leaders are unhealthy, so are their followers. People may teach what they know, but they reproduce what they are.

I once spoke at a conference with Larry Bossidy, the former CEO of Allied Signal (later Honeywell) and author of *Execution*. He touched on this dynamic between leaders and followers and spoke about the important role leaders have with their people. He said:

> The development of new leaders is not only the key to profitability; it is also very satisfying in terms of feeling like you've left a legacy,

not just an income statement. The question is often asked, "How am I doing as a leader?" The answer is how the people you lead are doing. Do they learn? Do they manage conflict? Do they initiate changes? You won't remember when you retire what you did the first quarter of 1994. What you will remember, is how many people you developed.

The best leaders are highly intentional about developing their people. Self-aware leaders are focused more on the success of their team members and organization than on their personal achievements or advancement. If their individual team members are growing and improving and their team is winning, they judge themselves successful.

REVEALING QUESTIONS TO ASK ABOUT TEAM MEMBERS

Earl Weaver, the former manager of the Baltimore Orioles, was known for continually baiting and arguing with umpires. One of the standard questions he asked of umpires in the first few innings of a game was, "Is it going to get any better, or is this as good as it's going to get?" That's a question every leader should ask himself. Why? Because the performance of the leader will greatly impact the performance of the team. Self-aware leaders don't wait for others to tell them whether they are successful. They take stock themselves. If you want to judge how you're doing as a leader, do so by asking the following four questions:

Question #1: Are the people on my team following me?

All leaders have two common characteristics: first, they are going somewhere; second, they are able to persuade other people to go with them. In a very practical sense, the second characteristic is what separates the real leaders from the pretenders. If someone with a leadership position has no followers, then that person may be called a leader, but isn't really leading. There is no such thing as a leader without followers!

It's important to note that having followers doesn't necessarily make individuals *good* leaders; it just makes them leaders. Pastor Stuart Briscoe tells the story of a young colleague who was officiating at the funeral of a war veteran. The dead man's military friends wanted to have some role in the service at the funeral home, so they requested that the pastor lead them down to the casket, stand with them for a solemn moment of remembrance, and then lead them out through the side door.

The young pastor did exactly that. There was only one problem: he picked the wrong door. With military precision, he marched the men into a broom closet. The whole group then had to beat a hasty, confused retreat, in full view of the mourners.[2]

When a leader knows where he is going and the people *know* that the leader knows where he is going, they begin to develop a healthy trust. This relationship of trust grows as the leader demonstrates continuing competence. Every time a good leader makes the right moves with the right motives, the relationship strengthens, and the team gets better.

> All leaders have two common characteristics: first, they are going somewhere; second, they are able to persuade other people to go with them.

Clarence Francis, who led the General Foods corporation in the 1930s and '40s, asserted, "You can buy a man's time; you can buy his physical presence at a given place; you can even buy a measured number of his skilled muscular motions per hour. But you cannot buy enthusiasm . . . you cannot buy loyalty . . . you cannot buy the devotion of hearts, minds or souls. You must earn these."

As a leader, you should never expect loyalty from others before you have built a relationship and earned trust. Demanding it up front seldom works. The loyalty of team members comes as a reward to the leader who earns it, not the one who yearns for it. The followership of the team is based not on position but on performance and motives. Successful leaders put the good of their people first. When they do this, they earn the respect of the team members, and they willingly follow them.

Question #2: Are my team members changing?

The second question you must ask to judge your leadership has to do with whether the people on your team are willing to make changes for the sake of progress. Progress does not occur without change. President Harry S. Truman commented, "Men make history and not the other way around. In periods where there is no leadership society stands still. Progress occurs when courageous, skillful leaders seize the opportunity to change things for the better."

Teams are able to seize opportunities only when team members are willing to change, and the burden of facilitating that falls most heavily on leaders. When team members trust leaders, they are willing to follow them into the unknown based on the promise of something better. Effective leaders are agents of change. They help to create a conducive environment for people to choose to do things differently or go in a new direction.

How do leaders facilitate this? First, they inspire others. Good leaders inspire their followers to have

> Good leaders inspire their followers to have confidence in *them*. Better leaders inspire their followers to have confidence in *themselves*.

confidence in *them*. Better leaders inspire their followers to have confidence in *them-selves*. This self-confidence lifts people's morale and gives them the energy to make the kinds of changes that will take them forward and improve their situation.

The other thing effective leaders do to promote change is create an environment of expectation. Jimmy Johnson, who coached the University of Miami to a national championship and the Dallas Cowboys to two Super Bowl victories, explained the importance of creating the right environment:

> My role as a head coach was to do three things: One, bring in people who are committed to being the very best; two, eliminate people who are not committed to being the very best; and three, the most important of my responsibilities, create an atmosphere where they could achieve their goals and the goals we set for our team. I wanted to put them in the right environment and delegate the responsibility so they could be the best they could be.[3]

People will become their best only if they are changing. And they are unlikely to change unless an effective leader is present to help facilitate the process.

Question #3: Are my team members growing?

Willingness to change on the part of the team can help an organization to improve, but for an organization to reach its highest potential, team members need to be willing to do more than just change. They need to keep growing.

Author Dale Galloway says, "The growth and development of people is the highest calling of a leader." I couldn't agree more. There is a lot of talk in the business community about finding and recruiting good people, and I acknowledge that it is important. But even if you find the best people you can, if you don't develop them, your competitor who *is* developing the people in their organization will soon pass you by.

The responsibility for developing people falls on the leader. And that means more than just helping people to acquire job skills. The best leaders help people with more than their jobs; they help them with their lives. They help them to become better *people*, not just better workers. They enlarge them. And that has great power because growing people create growing organizations.

Walter Bruckart, former vice president of Circuit City, remarked that the top five factors of excellence in

> "The growth and development of people is the highest calling of a leader."
> —DALE GALLOWAY

an organization are people, people, people, people, and people. I believe that is true, but only if you are helping those people to grow and reach their potential. And that's not always easy for a leader. It can exact a high price. As a leader, my success in developing others will depend upon the following:

- My high valuation of people—this is an attitude issue.
- My high commitment to people—this is a time issue.
- My high integrity with people—this is a character issue.
- My high standard for people—this is a goal-setting issue.
- My high influence over people—this is a leadership issue.

These core principles for people development are undergirded by a leader's belief in the people. If leaders don't believe in their people, their people won't believe in themselves. And if they don't believe in themselves, they won't grow. That may sound like a heavy weight of responsibility on a leader, but that's just the way it is. If the people aren't growing, it's a reflection on the leader.

Question #4: Are the members of my team succeeding?

Basketball coach Pat Riley, who has led two different teams to NBA championships, comments, "I think the ways a leader can measure whether or not he or she is doing a good job is 1) through wins or losses, 2) through the bottom line, 3) through the subjective and objective visual analysis of how individuals are improving and growing. If individuals are getting better results, I think the whole product is improving."[4] The bottom line in leadership is always results. Leaders may impress others when they succeed, but they impact others when the people on their team succeed. If a team, department, or organization isn't being successful, the responsibility ultimately falls on the leader.

It's been my experience that successful people who are not naturally gifted in leadership sometimes have a difficult time transitioning from achiever to leader. They are used to performing at a high level—doing tasks with excellence, reaching their goals, achieving financially—and they judge their progress by those things. When they become leaders, they often expect everyone else to perform at the level they did and to be self-motivated. And if the people on their team don't perform as expected, they ask, "What's wrong with them?"

Effective leaders think differently. They understand that they have a role in their followers' achievement and that their success as leaders is measured by the performance of their people. They take a hand in helping others perform at a high level. If they look at the people and see that they aren't following, changing, growing, and succeeding, they ask, "What's wrong with me?" and "What can I do differently to help the team win?"

> Leaders may impress others when they succeed, but they impact others when the people on their team succeed.

I love helping other people to succeed because I find it highly rewarding. I once received a note from Dale Bronner, a gifted leader that I mentored. In it he said:

> John, you have added value to me by exposing me to things I have not experienced, equipping me with resources to expand my mind, teaching me principles which serve as guardrails for my life and by providing me an avenue through which I can be accountable in a mentoring relationship. John, you have

provided something for my head, my heart and my hands which all make me a more valuable person to serve others.

That's the reason I lead and mentor others. Their success is my success. And the older I get, the more I enjoy seeing others succeed.

———

Leadership is meant to lift up others. Peter Drucker observed, "Leadership is the lifting of a man's vision to higher sights, the raising of a man's performance to a higher standard, the building of a man's personality beyond its normal limitations."[5] In other words, what Drucker was saying is, judge your leadership by the success of your team. If the men and women working with you are growing, improving, working together, and winning, then you're doing well as a leader.

THE SELF-AWARE LEADER'S QUESTIONS FOR REFLECTION

How successful is my team? In what ways should I take responsibility for their shortcomings, and how can I help them improve? How should I become a better leader?

_____

_____

_____

_____

_____

_____

_____

_____

_____

_____

_____

_____

ELEVEN

TAKE THE LONGER ROAD THAT LEADS TO HIGHER LEADERSHIP

....

In 1995, I faced one of the most difficult decisions of my life. I was twenty-six years into a highly successful career. I was in as good a position as I could be. I was forty-eight years old and at the top of my game. The church I was leading was at that time the "flagship" of the denomination, and it had a positive national reputation. I was respected, and I had influence not only in my own organization, but beyond it among other leaders in my profession. All that, plus I lived in San Diego, California, one of the most beautiful cities in the country. I was in an ideal situation—both financially and professionally. I believe I could have settled in there and stayed until I retired.

I had only one problem. I wanted to go to the next level as a leader. I wanted to reach and help new audiences of leaders both nationally and internationally, but I realized I couldn't do it if I stayed where I was. The next stage of growth would require me to give up my position, seek new and risky opportunities, and even move to another part of the country. I needed to face and answer a critical question: "Am I willing to give up all that I have for a new level of growth?"

THE ROAD TO A NEW LEVEL

That's a question that every leader must ask him- or herself more than once in a successful career. In *Leading Without Power*, Max De Pree writes, "By avoiding risk, we really risk what is most important in life—reaching toward growth, our potential, and a true contribution to a common goal."

I believe we human beings are always tempted to take the quick and easy route in life. We don't want to wait. We want instant gratification. But self-aware people understand the reality that everything worthwhile is uphill, and all roads to the places we most desire to go are long and require us to make trade-offs, to choose one thing over another.

I started learning this lesson about trade-offs as a child. My father would often admonish me by saying, "Pay now—play later." In fact, he said it a lot because I was someone who loved to play and *never* wanted to pay! What he was trying to teach me was to choose to do the difficult things first, so that I could enjoy the greater fruits of my labor later. I learned from him that we all pay in life. Anything we want will exact a price from us. The question is, "When will we pay?" Unfortunately, the longer we wait to pay, the greater that price. It is like interest that compounds. A successful life is a series of wise choices, to do hard things first and delay gratification. In my career, over and over I have traded security for opportunity. I've given up what many would consider an ideal position so that I could grow as a leader or make a bigger impact. I have always tried to make the choices that ultimately lead to the higher level of leadership.

> "By avoiding risk, we really risk what is most important in life—reaching toward growth, our potential, and a true contribution to a common goal."
> —MAX DE PREE

I've found that the higher we go in leadership, the harder it is to make trade-offs. Why? We have so much more to risk. People often tell dramatic stories about the sacrifices they had to make in the beginning of their careers. But the truth is that most of us had very little to lose in the beginning. The only thing of value that we have in the beginning is time. But the higher we climb, and the more we attain, the less we want to risk what we've gained. That's the reason many leaders climb only partway up the mountain of their potential and then stop. They come to a place where they are unwilling to give up something in order to get the next thing. As a result, they stall—some of them forever. And what's maybe even worse, they harm others with their decision to keep what they have. One of my mentors, author and consultant Fred Smith, said:

> Something in human nature tempts us to stay where we're comfortable. We try to find a plateau, a resting place, where we have comfortable stress and adequate finances. Where we have comfortable associations with people, without the intimidation of meeting new people and entering strange situations. Of course, all of us need to plateau for a time. We climb and then plateau for assimilation. But once we've assimilated what we've learned, we

climb again. It's unfortunate when we've done our last climb. When we have made our last climb, we are old, whether forty or eighty.

I'm seventy-four, and I don't know about you, but I never want to become that kind of old.

MAKE BETTER CHOICES

As I have traveled the road of leadership, I have always sought to make the better choice when I reached a fork in the road. Often, it was the longer slower path, but I felt certain it would allow me to reach a higher potential. I believe if you make similar choices throughout your career, it will make you a better leader and put you in a better position to help other people as you lead.

1. Choose Accomplishment Over Affirmation

When I started my career, I was a people pleaser. I wanted approval from my followers, admiration from my peers, and awards from my superiors. I was an affirmation junkie. But praises and accolades are like smoke that quickly fades away. Awards turn to rust. And financial rewards are quickly spent. At some point, I had to make a choice: Would I work to accomplish worthy tasks, or would I expend my energy trying to make myself look good? That decision gave me self-respect, caused others to respect me, and made me more valuable as a leader because I had more to give.

2. Choose Significance Over Security

Success does not mean simply being busy. What you give your life to matters. The great leaders in history were great not because of what they owned or earned but because of what they gave their lives to accomplish. They made a difference!

Staying where you are may give you security, but if what you're doing doesn't make a difference in the world and add value to people, it will never satisfy you. When you do work that really matters to you, it elevates you. It gives you a sense of purpose and satisfaction that makes you a better person and a better leader.

3. Choose Future Potential Over Financial Gain

One of life's ironies for me is that I was never motivated by money, yet Margaret and I ended up doing well financially. Why? I believe it was because I was always willing to put future potential ahead of financial gain.

The temptation is almost always to go for the bucks. But this goes back to my dad's advice to pay now, play later. If you are willing to sacrifice financially on the front end for the possibility of greater potential, you are almost always given greater chances for higher rewards—including financial ones.

4. Choose Personal Growth Over Immediate Gratification

If ever there was something our culture has a difficult time with, it is delayed gratification. If you look at
the statistics on how much debt people are in, and how
little they put into savings, you can see that most of us
tend to pursue immediate pleasure.

When I was a kid, school bored me, and I couldn't
wait to be done with it. I would have liked nothing better than to drop out, marry Margaret, my high school
sweetheart, and play basketball. But because I wanted
to have a career in leadership, I went to college, earned
my degree, and waited until after graduation to marry
Margaret. Those were a *very long* four years.

In "Become the Best Learner in the Room"
(Chapter 9) I told you about my experience with Curt
Kampmeier and how I became aware of the importance of personal growth. There have been many times
Margaret and I had to put off or sacrifice pleasures,
conveniences, or luxuries in order to pursue personal-
growth opportunities, but we've never regretted it. My
dedication to growth is what has allowed me to keep
leading for more than fifty years.

5. Choose Focus Over Further Exploration

Some people like to dabble. The problem with dab-
bling is that you never really become great at anything.
True, when you are young, you should try out new
things—see where your strengths and interests lie. But

the older you get, the more focused you should be. You can go far only if you specialize in something. I focus on leadership and communication. They are what I do best.

If you study the lives of great men and women, you will find that they were very single-minded. What one, two, or three things can you do better than anything else? Find them, and once you do, stick with them.

6. Choose Quality of Life Over Quantity of Life

I have to confess that I have a "more" mentality. If one is good, four is better. If somebody says he can hit a goal of twenty, I encourage him to reach for twenty-five. When I teach a one-hour leadership lesson, I want to put so much content in it that the people have a hard time taking notes. I want to add as much value as possible to them.

Because of this natural inclination, I've often had very little margin in my life. For years my calendar was booked solid, and I took very little time to relax. I remember once asking my brother and his wife to come visit me, and Larry replying, "No, you're too busy. If we come, we won't ever see you."

I once read that the president of a large publishing company sought out a wise man to get his advice. After describing the chaos that was his life, he silently waited to hear something of value from the sage. The older man at first said nothing. He simply took a teapot and began pouring tea into a cup. And he kept pouring until the tea overflowed and began to cover the table.

"What are you doing?" the businessman exclaimed.

"Your life," responded the wise man, "is like a teacup, flowing over. There's no room for anything new. You need to pour out, not take more in."

It has been very difficult for me to change my mindset from quantity to quality. Honestly, I'm still working on it. Having a heart attack in 1998 certainly made an impact on me in this area. So did having grandchildren. I now carve out more time for the really important things in my life. I suggest you do the same.

7. Choose Excellent Over Acceptable

This one is so obvious that it almost goes without saying. People do not pay for average. They are not impressed by anything that is merely acceptable. Leaders cannot rise on the wings of mediocrity. If something is worth doing, give it your best—or don't do it at all. Does it take longer to perform with excellence? Of course. Will it cost you more? Yes. But you will never regret giving your best.

8. Choose Multiplication Over Addition

When people make the shift from doer to leader, they greatly increase the impact that their lives can make. It is a significant jump because, as I assert in

The 17 Indisputable Laws of Teamwork, one is too small a number to achieve greatness. However, there is another jump that is more difficult and has even greater significance—changing from adder to multiplier.

> **Leaders who gather followers *add* to what they can accomplish. Leaders who develop leaders *multiply* their ability.**

Leaders who gather followers *add* to what they can accomplish. Leaders who develop leaders *multiply* their ability. How is that? For every leader they develop or attract, they gain not only that individual's horsepower but the horsepower of all the people that person leads. It has an incredible multiplying effect. All great leaders, regardless of where or when they lead, are leaders of leaders. To go to the highest level of leadership, you must learn to be a multiplier.

9. Choose a Second Half Over Another First Half

In his book *Halftime,* Bob Buford says that most people who are successful in the first half of their lives try to do the second half of their lives in the same way. What he's really saying is that they reach a plateau, and then they repeat their first half again. Why? Because it's much easier to stick with what's familiar.

Don't fall into that trap. When you get the chance, choose your second half. Don't just let a rerun of your first half happen. Once you have become successful, transition to doing something of *significance*. Invest in people. Do things that will live on after you are gone. If you are in the first half, keep paying the price so that you have something to offer in your second half. If you're in your second half, make the transition.

ARE YOU WILLING TO GIVE UP TO GO UP?

Being a good leader means being able to make good choices, not only for the members of your team, but for others. You have to let go of one thing in order to grasp a new one. People naturally resist that. We want to stay in our comfort zone—keep what's familiar. Sometimes circumstances are such that they force us to make a choice. But more often than not, if we want to make positive trades in our lives, we have to remain open to them.

During the Civil War, President Abraham Lincoln was asked by the army to raise an additional 500,000 recruits to fight. It was an action that was sure to be unpopular with the public. Lincoln's political advisors strongly recommended that he turn it down since they thought honoring the request would prevent his reelection. But Lincoln's decision was firm.

"It is not necessary for me to be reelected," he said,

"but it is necessary for the soldiers at the front to be reenforced by 500,000 men and I shall call for them. If I go down under the act, I will go down with my colors flying."

Lincoln is considered one of our greatest presidents because he was willing to make hard choices for the sake of the people he led and served. That is the kind of attitude all leaders need to possess. Every new level of growth we hope to experience as leaders calls for a new level of change. You cannot have one without the other. If you want to be a better leader, get ready to make some trades.

THE SELF-AWARE LEADER'S
QUESTION FOR REFLECTION

Where am I currently taking the shorter or easier road instead of making the more difficult choice that is likely to help my team or make me a better leader in the long run?

_____

_____

_____

_____

_____

_____

_____

_____

_____

_____

_____

_____

TWELVE

CREDIT OTHERS FOR YOUR SUCCESS

....

In 1998 Jeffrey Katzenberg and DreamWorks SKG produced an animated feature film called *The Prince of Egypt*. The movie was about Moses, who grew up in Egypt as a member of Pharaoh's household and eventually guided the children of Israel out of Egyptian bondage. As the movie was being made, the producers invited a few religious leaders to consult with them about it. I had the privilege of being one of those leaders. The experience was very enlightening to me as I was able to observe some of what happened behind the scenes during the making of that film.

As the opening date for the film approached, Margaret and I were delighted to receive an invitation to attend the premiere. What an exciting night it was! The evening was filled with laughter and words of congratulations. Yes, there was a red carpet, camera crews, media, interviews, and movie stars. And yes, Margaret and I walked on the red carpet and waved to the crowd—who ignored us.

When we were inside the theater and the movie began, I noticed how focused everyone was. Certainly a few of the attendees had seen the completed film, but most of them, like us, were seeing it for the first time. And they all had one question on their minds: "How did the movie turn out?"

As we watched, the people responded positively to seemingly insignificant things that a normal audience wouldn't. Why? Because they were involved in the details. It was a unique experience, and Margaret and I enjoyed it as well as the movie.

When the movie ended, the crowd applauded enthusiastically, and I quickly stood up to leave. Anyone who goes to an event with me knows that I like to exit early. Margaret quickly pulled me back down into my seat; nobody else in the theater had moved. Amazingly, excitement mounted as the credits began to roll. There were cheers as name after name rolled by, and the movie's stars were the main cheerleaders, as the many support people were recognized for their vital part in the success of the movie.

To the people in that theater, the credits were not just a bunch of random names. They represented the individual people they knew and cared about who had made specific contributions to *The Prince of Egypt*. Without these team members, successful completion of the film would not have been possible. That night I left with the impression that everyone was valued because everyone was valuable. It takes a lot of people to create a success. And it's a great reminder that as leaders, we need to credit others for our success.

NO SOLO LEADERS

I think sometimes there is a misconception that great leaders—especially the ones we read about from history—were able to accomplish big things regardless of what kind of help they received from others. We believe individuals like Alexander the Great, Julius Caesar, Charlemagne, William the Conqueror, Louis

> Without a lot of people working together, there would be no successful people.

XIV, Abraham Lincoln, and Winston Churchill would have been great no matter what kind of support they got. But that simply isn't true. Without a lot of people working together, there would be no successful people. Self-aware leaders recognize this truth.

Dan Sullivan and Catherine Nomura write in their book *The Laws of Lifetime Growth*:

> Only a small percentage of people are con-
> tinually successful over the long run. These
> outstanding few recognize that every success
> comes through the assistance of many other
> people—and they are continually grateful
> for this support. Conversely, many people
> whose success stops at some point are in that
> position because they have cut themselves
> off from everyone who has helped them.
> They view themselves as the sole source of
> their achievements. As they become more
> self-centered and isolated, they lose their
> creativity and ability to succeed. Continually
> acknowledge others' contributions, and you
> will automatically create room in your mind
> and in the world for much greater success.
> You will be motivated to achieve even more
> for those who have helped you. Focus on
> appreciating and thanking others, and the

conditions will always grow to support your increasing success.[1]

If you want to be a successful leader, you will need the support of many people. And if you are wise, you will appreciate and acknowledge them, crediting them for your success.

HELP FROM PEOPLE AHEAD OF ME

In the beginning years of my leadership journey I continually asked myself, "What can I accomplish?" My focus was too much on myself and what *I* could do. It didn't take long for me to discover that what I could accomplish on my own was quite insignificant. Self-made men don't make much. I quickly changed my question to be, "What can I accomplish *with others*?" I realized that success would be mine only if others helped me, and I helped them. Your team will never get ahead until your people are behind you, and that won't happen if you take all the credit.

> Your team will never get ahead until your people are behind you, and that won't happen if you take all the credit.

When I look back at all the people who have helped

me along over the years, I realize they fall into two main groups: mentors and supporters. Here's what's interesting about the mentors:

Some Mentors Who Never Knew Me Helped Me

I cannot count the number of mentors I've never met. How is that possible? They taught me through the books they've written or through biographies written about them. They've reached across time to instruct me, and their legacy lives on in me.

Some Mentors Who Knew Me Never Knew They Helped Me

Many people have been unconscious mentors by modeling principles of leadership and success that I have been able to apply to my life. I watched them and learned many of the things that now add value to my life. When I get the opportunity, it is my joy to express my gratitude to these unintentional mentors.

Some Mentors Knew Me and Knew They Helped Me

Many people have been intentional in their assistance to me. Some of them took me under their wing when I had no idea how much I didn't know. Others saw me as an emerging leader and guided me. Some today continue helping me to sharpen my thinking and improve as a leader. Most of the good things that happen to me are a direct result of their commitment to add value to me.

HELP FROM PEOPLE ALONGSIDE ME

While the mentors in my life often reached down to me to draw me up to where they were, the supporters often lifted me up and made me better than I was on my own. As I think about all the different kinds of people who have taken and continue to take that role with me, I recognize that most of them fall into one of several categories. I'll list them because you may find it helpful for identifying the kinds of people who are also helping you:

- **Time Relievers**—supporters who save me time
- **Gift Complementors**—supporters who do things I am not gifted to do
- **Team Players**—supporters who add value to me and my team
- **Creative Thinkers**—supporters who solve problems and give me options
- **Door Closers**—supporters who complete assignments with excellence
- **People Developers**—supporters who develop and raise up other leaders and producers
- **Servant Leaders**—supporters who lead with the right attitude
- **Mind Stretchers**—supporters who expand my thinking and my spirit
- **Relational Networkers**—supporters who bring other people into my life who add value to me

- **Spiritual Mentors**—supporters who encourage me in my faith walk
- **Unconditional Lovers**—supporters who know my weaknesses, yet love me unconditionally

I am so grateful to these people. I respect, value, and appreciate them. I could never be successful without them, and I let my current supporters know that on a daily basis. A Chinese proverb reads, "Behind an able man are always other able men [and women]." That has certainly been true in my life.

> **"Behind an able man are always other able men [and women]."**
> **—CHINESE PROVERB**

THE VISION DEPENDS ON OTHERS

I've had a lot of big dreams in my life. But God has never given me one that I could accomplish on my own. And because my dreams are always bigger than I am, I have only two choices: I can give up, or I can get help! I choose to ask for help. I have been blessed to be supported by the teams at the John Maxwell Company, EQUIP, the John Maxwell Team, and the John Maxwell Leadership Foundation (JMLF).

At seventy-four, I continue to pursue my dreams with the help of others. Currently, the JMLF is working in many countries around the world training facilitators to host Transformation Tables and teaching hundreds of thousands of people values in an effort to add value to them and help them live better lives. Thousands of coaches from the John Maxwell Team dedicate their time and pay their own expenses to travel to these countries as trainers. They are making a difference and helping others to change their world. They and my staff are the ones who deserve all the credit. Whatever success we see will be due to their efforts.

And that's true for all leaders, whether they lead giant corporations, own small entrepreneurial businesses, run non-profits, or lead a small team. The people on the team make everything work. The leader's job is to help them be successful.

When we understand this, we should express gratitude. The truth is that success is compounded when others join our cause. Followers make leaders possible. Good followers make it possible for there to be good leaders. If you never learn that lesson as a leader, your team members will resent you and your team will never reach the highest level of success. But if you give others the credit, you will become a better leader and you will lead a better team. People always appreciate working for someone who appreciates them.

THE SELF-AWARE LEADER'S
QUESTIONS FOR REFLECTION

Do I give my team members as much of the credit as I possibly can, or do I try to take some of the credit myself when we are successful? How can I change my attitude and express gratitude and appreciation for them every day?

_____

_____

_____

_____

_____

_____

_____

_____

_____

_____

_____

CONCLUSION

....

As you increase your self-awareness and gain experience as a leader, you understand more and more that leadership is not about you. It's about the team and helping them accomplish their mission.

Good leaders are facilitators of success. They use their talents and influence to clear the way for their team members and help them succeed. Self-aware leaders never pretend to be perfect, to have all the answers, or to lack weaknesses. They use whatever strengths they have to help the team; they ask others to help them in areas of weakness. Together they move forward.

As you embrace and practice the lessons in this book, my hope is that you will become better at knowing yourself, leading yourself, and interacting with your team members. While self-awareness is a lifelong journey, with each step you take in knowing yourself, the better able you will be at leveraging your strengths and focusing on developing a leadership style that suits who you are. When you have the confidence to be yourself and allow your team members to be themselves, together you can become the team you were always meant to be.

NOTES

....

Chapter 1: Become Good at Leading Yourself
  1. Walt Kelly, "Pogo," "We Have Met the Enemy . . . and He Is Us," https://www.kshs.org/kansapedia /pogo-comic-strip/15641, accessed 19 March 2021.
  2. Proverbs 22:7 (NIV).
  3. Sam Rayburn, https://www.nytimes.com/1973/01 /26/archives/the-man-and-his-humor-are-recalled .html, accessed 19 March 2021.

Chapter 2: Know and Work Within Your Strengths
  1. Erik Sherman, "Think You Know Your Competitive Advantage? Maybe Not," Inc.com, 11 September 2014, https://www.inc.com/erik -sherman/think-you-know-your-competitive -advantage-maybe-not.html.

2. Marcus Buckingham and Donald O. Clifton, *Now Discover Your Strengths* (New York: The Free Press, 2001), 6.

3. Frances Hesselbein, *Hesselbein on Leadership* (New Jersey: Wiley & Sons, 2002), 79.

Chapter 3: Put Your Team Ahead of Your Own Career Advancement

1. John White, "Here Are the Top 7 Reasons People Get Fired (Are You Guilty of Any of Them?)," Inc.com, 29 December 2016, https://www.inc.com /john-white/here-are-the-top-7-reasons-people -get-fired-are-you-guilty-of-any-of-them.html.

Chapter 4: Look at Yourself When People Quit

1. Malcolm Gladwell, *Blink: The Power of Thinking Without Thinking* (New York: Little, Brown, and Company, 2005), 18–34.

2. Paul J. Zak, "The Neuroscience of Trust," *Harvard Business Review*, January–February 2017, https:// hbr.org/2017/01/the-neuroscience-of-trust, accessed 19 March 2021.

Chapter 5: Listen More than Talk

1. Jim Lange, *Bleedership* (Mustang, OK: Tate, 2005), 76.

2. Lorin Woolfe, *The Bible on Leadership: From Moses to Matthew—Management Lessons for*

Contemporary Leaders (New York: AMACOM, 2002), 103–104

Chapter 6: Handle Criticism with Grace

1. Ken Blanchard, Spencer Johnson, *The One-Minute Manager* (New York: William Morrow & Co., 1982).

Chapter 7: Admit Your Mistakes and Learn from Them

1. Michael Abrashoff, *It's Your Ship: Management Techniques from the Best Damn Ship in the Navy* (New York: Warner Business, 2002), 33.
2. The statement "All generalizations are false including this one" is originally attributed to Mark Twain.
3. Abrashoff, *It's Your Ship*, 91–92.

Chapter 8: Stop Micromanaging Others and Start Managing Your Priorities

1. Kevin Kruse, "The 80/20 Rule and How It Can Change Your Life," Forbes.com, https://www.forbes.com/sites/kevinkruse/2016/03/07/80–20-rule/.
2. Barry Conchie, "The Demands of Executive Leadership: What Separates Great Leaders from All the Rest?," *Gallup Management Journal*, 13 May 2004, ttps://news.gallup.com/businessjournal/11614/seven-demands-leadership.aspx.

3. Stan Toler and Larry Gilbert, *Pastor's Playbook: Coaching Your Team for Ministry* (Kansas City: Beacon Hill Press, 1999).

Chapter 10: Judge Your Leadership by the Success of Your Team

1. Ronald Reagan, second presidential debate with incumbent Jimmy Carter, 28 October 1980, https://www.youtube.com/watch?v =loBe0WXtts8, accessed 19 March 2021.

2. Stuart Briscoe, *Everyday Discipleship for Ordinary People* (Colorado Springs: Scripture Press, 1988), 28.

3. Jimmy Johnson, https://www.thelimbaughletter .com/thelimbaughletter/august_2017/Mobile PagedArticle.action?articleId=1134899 #articleId1134899, accessed 19 March 2021.

4. Pat Riley, "The Pat Riley Formula for a Winning Team," *Selling Power*, 2 Feb. 2010, https://www .sellingpower.com/2010/02/02/3528/the-pat-riley -formula-for-a-winning-team, accessed 19 March 2021.

5. Peter Drucker, quoted in "You're No Leader—At Least Not Without Practice," The Drucker Institute, 23 Oct. 2011, https://www.drucker .institute/thedx/youre-no-leader-at-least-not -without-practice/, accessed 19 March 2021.

Chapter 12: Credit Others for Your Success

1. Dan Sullivan and Catherine Nomura, *The Laws of Lifetime Growth: Always Make Your Future Bigger Than Your Past* (San Francisco: Berrett-Koehler, 2006), 43.

ABOUT THE AUTHOR

....

John C. Maxwell is a #1 *New York Times* bestselling author, speaker, coach, and leader who has sold more than thirty-four million books in fifty languages. He has been called the #1 leader in business and the most influential leadership expert in the world. His organizations—the John Maxwell Company, the John Maxwell Team, EQUIP, and the John Maxwell Leadership Foundation—have translated his teachings into seventy languages and have used them to train millions of leaders from every country in the world. A recipient of the Horatio Alger Award and the Mother Teresa Prize for Global Peace and Leadership from the Luminary Leadership Network, Dr. Maxwell influences *Fortune* 500 CEOs, the presidents of nations, and entrepreneurs worldwide. For more information visit JohnMaxwell.com.